New and Collected Poems, 1970-1985

David Ignatow

New and
Collected Poems,
1970-1985

Wesleyan University Press
Middletown, Connecticut

Some of these poems were first published in *Abraxas, Agni Review, The American Poetry, American Poetry Review, Amicus Journal, Antaeus, Arion's Dolphin, Arts in Society, The Atlantic Monthly, Blacksmith, boundary 2, Butt, Centennial Review, Changes, Chicago Review, Chicago Tribune, Choice, Colorado State Review, Columbia Forum, Confrontation, Crazy Horse, Dacotah Territory, Denver Quarterly, Epoch, Equal Time, The Face of Poetry, Field, The Georgia Review, Granite, Gravida, Grilled Flowers, The Hampden-Sydney Poetry Review, Harper's Magazine, Harvard Magazine, Hawaii Literary Review, The Hudson Review, Images, Intrepid, Ironwood, Kayak, Kenyon Review, Lemming, Lillabulero, Little Caesar, Madrona, Manhattan Review, Mill Mountain Review, Modern Poetry Series, Modern Poetry Studies, Moons and Tailes, Mouth, The Nation, New Letters, News of the Universe, The New York Quarterly, The New York Times, Next, The Niagara Magazine, The North Stone Review, Occasional Papers #9, The Ohio Review, Ontario Review, Organ, Paideuma, Paris Review, Partisan Review, Pequod, Plainsong, Ploughshares, Poetry, Poetry East, Poetry Magazine, The Poetry Miscellany, Poetry Now, Portland Review Magazine, Quest/77, Quest/80, Rapport, San Marcos Review, Seneca Review, Shankpainter, The Sole Proprietor, Some, Southern Poetry, Sou'wester, Street, Sumac, Sun, Survivor's Manual, Tennessee Poetry Journal, Transatlantic Review, Underground Rag Mag, Unmuzzled Ox, Vanderbilt Poetry Review, Virginia Quarterly.*

Facing the Tree, Tread the Dark and *Whisper to the Earth* were first published by *Atlantic Monthly Press. Leaving the Door Open* was first published by *The Sheep Meadow Press.*

Library of Congress Cataloging-in-Publication Data

Ignatow, David, 1914–

New and collected poems, 1970–1985.

(Wesleyan poetry)

I. Title. II. Series.

PS3517.G53N49 1986   811'.54   85–15311

ISBN 0-8195-5115-5 (alk. paper)

ISBN 0-8195-6117-7 (pbk. : alk. paper)

All inquiries and permissions requests should be addressed to the Publisher, Wesleyan University Press, 110 Mt. Vernon Street, Middletown, Connecticut 06457.

Distributed by Harper & Row Publishers, Keystone Industrial Park, Scranton, Pennsylvania 18512.

Manufactured in the United States of America

FIRST EDITION

WESLEYAN POETRY

Contents

Whisper to the Earth   149

Facing the Tree

To Nicanor Parra,
Wherever he is
Whatever he must do
In the service
of his poetry

■ *Invocation*

Dirt and stone, if I may know you as you know yourselves,
if you do have sense of yourselves,
I walk upon and study you as my next brothers and sisters,
in this only way I know how to think about you.
I pick you up in my hands and run you slowly through my
    fingers,
I feel so close to you, if only not to fear
but to know and make you my kin, even if I must do it alone.

I am resigned, if I must say it that way.
Try as I might, I cannot think myself exactly that.
I see us each in separate worlds
and because I must join yours and gradually become as you,
I want to know what home will be like there.

If I could say that from you can be made men and women,
how happy and relieved I'd be to know
we have a sort of exchange program between us,
in which we spring up out of the dust
and are greeted with open arms to tell that all is well
back there growing its fruits.
And then to embrace, all of us together,
and celebrate with drink and dancing
and to see one into the soil
with solemn benedictions on a current of joy,
waving him farewell as he disintegrates to dust.

I speak to you in pity for myself; speak to me
and return the love I must have for you,
since I must be buried one day in you
and would go toward love again, as in life.
Let us be reconciled to one another.
Dirt and stone into which my flesh will turn,

this much we have in common. As I cannot speak to my bones
nor my blood nor my own flesh, why then must I speak?
What says I must speak if I am not answered?
What then that I should speak or am I speaking at all,
if my own flesh and bones cannot answer me,
as if already they were partners of the stones and dirt?

■ *Reading the Headlines*

I have a burial ground in me where I place the bodies
without fuss or emotion, hundreds of thousands at a glance.
I stow them in and as it happens I am eating dinner.
I continue to eat, feeding myself and the dead.

I walk around in this burial ground, examining it
with curiosity, find it dark but stroll with a sense
of safety, my own place. I want to lie down in it,
dissatisfied with it, true, but seeing no exit, I lie
down to rest and dream.

I am lost anyway, without horizon or recognizable features.
It's just to walk on. At least it's not necessary
to kill myself. I'll die of attrition of my energy to live.

I know my direction and have companions, after all.

■ *I'm Here*

The radio said, Go to your shelters,
in such a low whisper that we stood there
in front of the set, not wanting to understand
it was not part of a play. The color
of the blast came high over the horizon.
We stood watching it, still unable to realize
we were being killed, for real.

We ran and are still running, it seems,
though our bodies have long since dropped
from us. We could be the wind rushing
through the trees or the stars moving out
to the perimeter. We know we felt ourselves
vanishing in flame and wind,
and it seemed as though we were becoming
one or the other.

How then can we still speak to you
without body or voice? Do you know
there is another world, very silent,
which penetrates the one you're in?
Without your knowledge or your feeling it,
you hear my every word but do not see
or feel me anywhere. I have no sight
or touch of you either yet speak
because I am from nowhere in particular.
And now can you tell me what it is to live?

Are you lying in a cave at rest?
Or waiting crouched for the enemy,
or do you have your family with you still,
comforting them with food?
What is your situation?

Once having been human like you, if I may presume
nothing for you has changed in form, body
or mind, I hunger for a voice to fill
an emptiness in my speech,
which perhaps is what makes me invisible.
You can speak to me by standing perfectly still
where you are and breathing regularly.
Then I'll understand that all is well
for the human and, content, vanish.

■ *Letter to a Friend*

Yesterday I killed a man. It was such a surprise to me. I was driving along in my car, taking it easy, stopping at red lights and in a leisurely way starting up, knowing the next light was timed to turn red before I could reach it.

I was not racing, I was not impatient. I was not trying to do the unusual or unexpected, when as if from beneath the pavement he sprang up in front of my car. Was it from beneath? I'm too dazed to know and almost delighted at being completely innocent in the law.

They say that where I ran him down the tar is ripped open as if he might have torn through from beneath, but he's dead and no one can explain.

There's no sewer below from which to spring; just plain dirt that once was farmland, not so long ago. I was here when the pavement was laid down. Could it have been the farmer who sold the land, protesting after taking the money, his conscience bothering him? Or a fertility god? I don't believe in such things.

Could I have been dreaming at the wheel? Had this man been lying in the road already hurt, unable to rise quickly and I caught up in thought, the ride going smoothly?

But why should I question myself? I did right, I stopped the car, I got out and ran back to pick him up, and as I raised his head it began to come apart in my hand like the broken head of a doll. I put it right back on the ground, I called the police, they questioned me for hours, I answered patiently, convinced of my innocence, and I was released.

They smiled at each other, as if they knew something they would not tell me. At least I'm innocent and I have killed a man. What a curious sensation. I wonder if it will ever happen again.

My President Weeps

The President's blood is on my hands; he has taken another decision, this time to smash the dikes. His life is full of weeping in self-pity at the cruelties he must impose, and blood pours from his eyes at the intensity of grief. Standing beside him, with my hands reaching to comfort him, they are covered with his blood, but he pushes me off and is harsh, telling me to leave or be killed too. I leave.

He does not know I already am dead. He has taken the position that all must die and he has taken the position knowingly and has built it out of thoughts about freedom and independence and the rights of man. Such a President who lingers in the gardens of the future to pluck one flower that he could bring to life.

Blood covers him entirely from his weeping eyes. My President, my poems that are stained with blood, poems in which the blood runs down the page, poems that have holes in them the size of shrapnel wounds, poems that peel off from paper like napalmed skin, poems that crumple together like the gassed, poems that eat themselves in agony like village animals, their guts hanging out in the rice fields after bombing. My President weeps and weeps and I tear my arms from their sockets, my fingers from their joints, my hair from its roots, my eyes from their cavities to tell you my President weeps and looks darkly back at us from the television.

■ *I Wonder Who Is Next*

Listen, Mao Tse-tung will live forever; they are giving him a lung transplant, he smokes too much, and a heart transplant, and all his other organs are under acupuncture. They keep an eye on his pulse and watch his every fragile move. When he speaks they record his voice for significant variations and his handwriting is scrutinized. Wherever he walks or sits they surround him in a crowd from head to foot. He becomes invisible. Live forever, Mao Tse-tung.

▪ My Enemies

I know how I have learned to hate. I've turned on trees and animals and crushed the ant in my path. Many a time I've ignored the sun and the moon in my walk to keep my eyes turned down toward the dirt of the path or its concrete and often refused to wash my body of its sweat and oils. I saw no purpose in a tree growing or in the food set before me. I could see no commerce between men and me. Did the stars touch each other? Did they reach out to give light when the light failed in another? Was the sun sympathetic? Did the moon care? Did my feet warn me of the creatures beneath their soles as I walked? Who held me in such regard as to want to unburden me of my faults and let me live? It was a concert of divisiveness without any particular foe or intention: a salad of kinds of separateness on which I was fed, and because I lived I wondered about all this and remarked on my living. Why, I asked myself, was it not possible to name the faults and hold them as a keepsake for the living? I did this and I survived my pain and everything about the sun was granted for what it was and everything about my parents and my brothers, my food and the soles of my shoes and the separateness of stars and the purpose lacking in the trees and my own divisiveness. Granting all this and knowing that I had brought my own death closer by living this day I thought of such a thing as love to describe it.

I greet the hair on my head, chest and pubic region each morning as my companions in living. I expose my teeth to welcome them in my mouth, teeth that stay with me out of loyalty or their own desire to remain and be. I am prepared now for loving the day. I can be hurt and I brood.

I may take my quiet revenge but hurt and brooding and revenge absorb me more deeply in this meaning, that my life loves my toenails even as I love my enemies.

■ The fork I raise to my mouth should be the fork in a dream; the kiss I give should be the kiss given in a dream. The dream I would be having would be of the world being dreamed as it should be: of sequences, the creator at the center—me who could dream the world or not but with preference for the dream flowing, enchanting in the ease it could be lived or turned off: the feel of a fork in my hand like that of silk. In the world where the steel for it is made the fork is hard and pointed. How may I live in silkiness until the dream brings me to a death entered with a silky ease?

■ *The Diner*

If I order a sandwich and get a plate of ham and eggs instead, has communication broken down? Is there a chef in the house? There's no chef. I get only silence. Who brought me the ham and eggs? I was sitting at the counter when it arrived. I don't remember anyone bringing it. I'm leaving right now to find another place to eat in, a bit more congenial than this silence, with no one to witness that I ordered exactly what I say I did. But now the door is closed and I can't leave.

Will someone please open the door, the one who gave me the ham and eggs instead of a sandwich? If I'm dissatisfied and want to leave why must I stay? Can the proprietor do as he pleases with anyone on his property? Am I his property too? What do you know! I have to eat what's given me or go hungry. I have to be nice about it too and say thank you to the silence. But I want to know why I can't have what I want that's such an innocent wish as between a sandwich and a plate of ham and eggs? What have I said or did I say what I thought I did or am I in my own country where my language is spoken? Where am I? Why can't I leave this diner? This is not my country. I don't belong here. I never even got a passport to come. I don't remember leaving. I don't remember crossing the border and I'm the only guy here at the counter. Something phony is going on. Somebody is trying to drive me nuts or rob me or kill me. I want to go back where I came from. I was on the road hungry, driving. It was dark and I hadn't eaten my dinner.

You know, it's quite possible I made these ham and eggs myself instead of a sandwich. It may be I'm the owner because no one else is here and I have the key to open the door, exactly like my car key. I must have arranged it that way. Now when in hell did I buy this diner and who needs it!

■ *The Assassin*

Stare into the gun barrel, a wildly grinning man behind it, and think twice; first to save yourself, next to reconcile yourself to dying. Plead for your life and offer treasures of your soul: your human love, recognition of his life, your wish to know him as a person. He slowly squeezes at the trigger, satisfied that what he's heard is nonsense to a man who knows this is the way to prove himself a human like the others. His eyes widen, lips slowly open to speak or to swallow. A noise, you're hit: your life inside intensifies, you cannot stop yourself from falling at his feet. Your head is drained of strength, a peace is filling it. You lift your face to let him see what he too can expect one day as a blessing, and your eyes close on his amazed expression.

▪ *Talking to Myself*

About my being a poet, the trees certainly haven't expressed an interest, standing at a distance. I'd expect that at least they'd try to learn something new besides growing their leaves, old stuff by now, and anyway it's done by so many others. Wouldn't these trees want to know what they'll be doing in a hundred years, what they look like now, how they stand, what's their name, where they are and what they actually do in winter and in summer, deaf, dumb and happy as they are? Not happy, simply willing to go on as always. Not even willing, just doing what comes naturally. To them I might as well be dead or a tree.

To stay among the trees as if I were at home, arrived from a long journey, I am digging a place for a burial with my feet.

■ Now Celebrate Life and Death

Croatian guerrillas executed in Yugoslavia.
—News report

The Croatians watching the soldiers line up in front of them for the execution and then feeling the bullets enter their heads and chests, does this have anything in common with the man who inserts his penis into the vagina where he also feels himself while the woman feels herself? Did the Croatians live for the shots to enter and the man for his penis to enter in order for the woman to feel herself a body, therefore a being, a person she would want herself to be called then, very pleased and flattered that she had made the man feel himself in her as the man is pleased that he can make her feel herself through him: giving each other to confirm bodily existence? And so how should the Croatians feel toward their executioners and the executioners toward their victims? Can each take pride in the others' bodily feelings arising from actions each must perform? May they give thanks to each other, the executioners for feeling their power to kill and exercising it with efficiency and terror, finally feeling guilty but thankful, for without feeling they do not exist. The executed, as they sink to their knees bullet-laden, may thank the firing squad for having given them to feel their identity this intensely at its last moments. So eat and fill your mouth and discover the response in yourself, you becoming aware of taste buds that please your palate that make your body you. Now celebrate life and death for this reason.

■ Information

This tree has two million and seventy-five thousand leaves.
Perhaps I missed a leaf or two but I do feel triumphant
at having persisted in counting by hand branch by branch
and marked down on paper with pencil each total.
Adding them up was a pleasure I could understand;
I did something on my own that was not dependent on others,
and to count leaves is not less meaningful than to count
the stars, as astronomers are always doing. They want the
facts to be sure they have them all. It would help them to
know whether the world is finite. I discovered one tree
that is finite. I must try counting the hairs on my head,
and you too. We could swap information.

■ Make up a poem about a man going to sleep in his business clothes to wake up in a hospital in a pair of regulation hospital pajamas. He demands to be let out but they tell him he fell asleep on the job and so must have something wrong with him. He insists nothing is wrong. He was tired and that was all. How can it be tiredness only, they insist, when he let the phone ring all day and night while sleeping in his chair at the desk? It was only when his wife came looking for him in panic that he was discovered. "Did I let the phone ring all day and night?" "Yes," they reply gently to mark their concern for him and to let him know he's under their care. "Well, perhaps I wanted to," he replies vigorously, and starts to climb out of bed. They forcefully restrain him and he begins to shout. "But we have taken a cardiogram of your heart while you were asleep and it exhibited a dangerous slowness." "I was hibernating," he shouts. "We took a reading of your brain waves and they were virtually still." "I was hibernating. I was a bear and now I am a man again!" Oh, then he is insane, they tell each other with their eyes and insanity is the cause. We can't let him go back to his business. "You are not feeling well," they tell him softly, holding him tightly to the bed. "Of course I am insane!" he shouts. "So what of it! I want to be insane. I'm entitled to be insane, if I want to be! I'll even shit in this bed to prove it to you. Nothing can stop me and if you don't release me I'll have to harm myself to prove to you that freeing me is the better policy." His logic is distorted, they decide and find no choice within themselves but to keep him under restraint. "Then you don't want to go back to your business?" they probe to prove to him that he is not fit to lead a normal life. "But I do want to go back to my business! I do want to run it as I've always done and I've always been insane! My business permits me to be insane, in fact encourages me and supports me and nourishes my insanity, so what the hell, you're holding back a good man." They are baffled. What kind of disease is this? They have to think, but first they have to tie him down with straps to secure him to the bed, after which they leave to consult among themselves in private, and they think they have had a very queer experience themselves, listening to his logic and conviction. They have to laugh. Out of insanity, he had said, he had founded his business, made it profitable for himself. Is it a way to live, they wonder, and the question remains un-answered because their own lives already seem peculiar to them but enjoyable, having to deal with this kind of patient who makes them sense their own peculiar condi-tion, to have to dwell on him. Are they insane in their way and is it dangerous while enjoyable or it is dangerous because it is enjoyable? They put themselves in a com-plete dilemma about it but accept it as a dilemma, which spurs them on, fed on the occupation they have chosen, which, they could concede, has its own logic. Their faces betray no horror. They mean to keep on and would resist any attempt within themselves or from the patient to con-demn their practise and seek his release.

■ *A Triptych*

I

As you hold off the mugger who never knew you, never met you, never suffered through your deeds, everything is fine, you scream, as you kick him in the groin and then swing your foot straight up into his belly to lay him out unconscious. He dies—internal hemorrhage. Cops open notebooks in their hands, their faces bent upon the page, suspicious, apathetic, indifferent and displeased to have to think of you, a stranger. You have a kind of stranglehold upon their thought, you've blocked their easy breathing in the night. They take you in, they want to know what were you doing on the street the very moment that the mugger showed himself. Open your life, how when you spoke last to your wife it was to tell her the world extended in so many directions from the house. That does it and you're booked. One turns and grabs you by the throat and you stand together at the sergeant's desk to round out the world.

2

"Out of evil cometh good." Let me think now: the strangler will have picked my pockets, about ten dollars. He will have had the satisfaction of getting away with it again and be able to buy himself a new fix. My wife will collect on my insurance and clear the mortgage on the house. I think she will cry for days, as will my daughter. I don't know about my son, he may think about the dangers of walking the streets at night. Do I want to die to hasten these events?

I know the city will survive my death, and when I consider that policemen are needed at their posts and mailmen must continue to deliver their mail of welfare checks and prize announcements, and funerals must be held and bodies buried to keep the smell and infestation from the living, all's well about my dying. I wonder then that I hesitate to submit to his hands. I too must carry on as

usual which is my peace: the trains on time, the meal
served when needed, the water on tap and grass, trees and
birds as I require them, everything in its place: death,
love, happiness, warmth and job security. I'm all for
them. Kill me when you must, mugger.

3

I should believe that a man being mugged in his own
apartment is part of the order of things. I'm sad about
this, one of the last among the non-mugged, an old order
vanishing into hospitals. Should I turn mugger too, writ-
ing about it in secret between jobs? I see a still younger
generation on the horizon standing in armies waiting to
advance. We of the earlier order of muggers would then
have to salute as they attack us and pray they prosper
in their trade and learn to be outraged when they are
mugged in turn to feel themselves estranged in their own
land or have escaped north among the Eskimos who wear
thick gloves and cannot mug efficiently.

CODA

A man sitting on the ground with his head in his hands,
he no longer understands himself. His body forms an en-
closure; his head in his hands is his world, he holds his
world in his hands and it feels the pressure of his fingers
in despair. When he dies it will be as if he has gone to
live, and so he lies back upon the ground, his one other
abiding contact, and is at peace, having given himself.

■ I could spend my life contemplating the weaving back and forth of the topmost branches with no visible force moving them. I could imagine they do this of their own free will. I know a log is lying across two stones to make a bench but to sit upon it is to confirm this knowledge. I know that a bullet shot out of a gun can pierce the heart but to confirm it I would have to pull the trigger aimed at you, only for the sake of knowledge. I know nothing beyond this method to help me know.

II

■ *In a Dream*

at fifty I approach myself,
eighteen years of age,
seated despondently on the concrete steps
of my father's house,
wishing to be gone from there
into my own life,
and I tell my young self,
Nothing will turn out right,
you'll want to avenge yourself,
on those close to you especially,
and they will want to die
of shock and grief. You will fall
to pleading and tears of self-pity,
filled with yourself, a passionate stranger.
My eighteen-year-old self stands up
from the concrete steps and says,
Go to hell,
and I walk off.

■ *Thinking*

I am caught in the body of a fish.
If I am the fish itself this speech
is the sound of water escaping
through my gills and like all fish
I will be caught in the mouth
of a larger one or be netted
or die of being fish. Thinking
that I am caught inside, a person
with a right to freedom as I've been
trained to think, my thought is another
kind of net because this right
to freedom is a torment like being
caught in the body of a fish.

■ Biography

In these typewriter keys is the story of my parents and me
that I will not give the keys to type,
the three of us held in tension
I do not want interrupted,
unable to resolve the differences between us
and they are dead.

■ The Weather

Live for myself
said the wind
Live for myself
said the rain
Live for myself
said the night
I bent my head
turned up my collar

■ My poetry is for the night
of empty buses. I write,
depleted, and hug my death.
Live for others, I hear whispered,
for the child growing,
face of a rushing stream.

I fall asleep
as it were a poem
being written
to resolve my cares
into a final solution
and as my eyes close
and silence spreads itself
inside me like a wave
I know I am succeeding,
and in sleep rejoice.

■ There must be something wrong with me
wanting to keep going through
the endless griefs as if I had iron
bowels and a stone head
and perhaps it is stone and iron
in me now thinking.

■ *My Own Line*

I try to follow through the maze
by holding on with both hands
and slowly threading, picking out the knots
and tangles. Sometimes when I disentangle them
I stand confused, looking around for what is mine
and can't find it and am lost and panicky,
so many look alike, so many more tempting
in color and strength and others taut
and keen. I am afraid of them, incapable
of handling any, adapted only to my own
these many years, and when I find it
at the bottom of the heap
or somewhere in the middle, gray colored,
obscured almost, I grab it in relief,
freed of my uncertainty and hang on
grimly and move ahead through the whirring
jungle of lines above, beneath and around me,
gnashing my teeth in hope
to find my way out into the clear
to where my line is leading,
slack at both ends.

■ *The Refuse Man*

I'm going to pull my stinking wagon
through the streets and countryside,
letting it smell up the highways
and its odor crawl into the one-
and two-family houses along the road
and over the corn and wheat fields
and let the cows raise their heads
from munching to bellow their anger
and the cop to draw up alongside
my wagon—I'll be pulling it
between the shafts—and let this cop,
holding his nose, come over to ask
in an awed voice what the hell
it is I'm hauling and I'll tell him,
as sweetly as I can, "A dish of rotted guts,
an empty skull, a fetid breast, a swarming
belly, a corpse, a man right out
of his mother's belly given his occupation,
and I've put myself between the shafts—
a horse will not come near this;
I had to, being a man."

■ *In This Dream*

a vacuum cleaner held over my head
is drawing out my brains through my nostrils,
blood running in a column straight up
into the vacuum bag whining like a jet engine.
I feel my intestines too beginning to move up
through my gullet and soon they will be pouring
through my nose. My bones quiver in their sockets,
my knees are shaking. I sit down,
emptiness is becoming me. I can no longer think,
I just listen to the sucking vacuum.
Here goes my heart, straight up into my throat
and choking me, pumping in my throat.
It is filling my mouth, it is forcing its way
between my teeth. The vacuum roars
and my mouth flies open and my heart is gone.

How is it I keep writing?
The vacuum roars and whines alternately,
my ears stick to my head but now my head
is rising, a wind is whistling through my skull.
My head is being lifted from my neck.
Take me altogether, great vacuum:
my arms, legs, sex, shoes, clothes,
my pen gripped in my whitened hand
drained of blood. Take me altogether
and I triumph, whirled in the vacuum bag
with my satellite heart, brain, bones and blood.

■ Said a voice to me
from the pillow
Ho Ho I am Bill Williams
Write me a poem
about yourself
Are you afraid?
Get it down
say it say it say it

I lifted my head
dazed
my stomach turning
grey dawn at the window
my senses flowing back on me
swinging me over and over
over and under an ocean
isolating me
from wife and child

■ *Backyard*

When I wake up in the morning I'm scattered
over a gray landscape, my arms and legs
immobilized. I don't see the connection
between myself and a finch warbling
in the rising sun. I want
an explanation of the world.

Catbird complaining in the sun
for something nobody knows what.
He flies away, can't make himself understood
like other birds. He'll settle for bugs
as they come out of hiding
after rain.

▪ *Spinning*

I hold my hands out to you
but you say your hands
do not exist. You also say
that I do not have hands,
that I have an illusion of hands
and that speaking to you
is speaking to myself,
appealing to myself
to be at one with me.
You show me what you mean
by spinning, standing
in one place—a humming top.
It delights you
and you urge me on.
I begin to turn
as I begin to weep.

■ Where is a rock to bore a hole through?
I need to find a rock to drill
a look through to the other side.
Any rock, any ordinary species.
I'll be happy with a rock.

■ *With My Back*

With my back to the insane world
of the next room I look into my poetry
for the gentleness in making do
with the known facts. On his side
of the wall sits a young man
spilling fear from his mouth.
I read in my poetry that fear teaches
me to love and that love also
is the beginning of fear
so that I find myself upon a cutting edge.
He in the room next door is bloody.
I look in my poetry for what to do
to help and read I must remain
absolutely still. He must be allowed
to think he is alone and that the world
waits on him for decision.

■ *The Future*

I am going to leave a child in an empty room.
She will have my body to look down on
at my death, when she will ask of the room
its address, the room silent,
stretching across the sky.
What comfort for her, my only expectation,
as in her infancy she climbs upon my lap?

My daughter, as I recede into the past,
I give you this
worth more than money,
more than a tip on the market:
keep strong;
prepare to live without me
as I am prepared.

■ Birds in Winter

At the command
they rise trembling on air
and fly off in formation.
Offspring will return
who cannot be told
from their parents.

■ Peace

Peace belongs with the birds,
buffeted by wind,
driven close to the wave's lash.
They have found a place
for storms in their brain;
utter no protest,
their wings widespread.

■ Somehow it does not write itself, our life together,
my need expressed by your giving,
my seeking satisfied with your finding.
Truly we fit like bolt in lock,
to keep our house free of childishness and pretension;
love not in rhetoric,
emotion not in eyes.
When I feel your leg thrown over me in sleep
I say, That is the thought.

III

■ He moves straight before him, legs moving lightly
over ground. Encounters a lamppost
with caressing hands, moves on
to meet a water hydrant he lightly vaults,
eyes lifted to the tall buildings
irregular in height. Smiling as if amused
in sleep he climbs rapidly up one wall.
Tenants sip their coffee and look down
into the street or from the window talk
to someone in the room. He nears the very top
of one skyscraper, lifts a window and steps in
and strides to the other end of the room
and through its wall. Around him conversation
never stops, an office of whirring typewriters.
In the corridor, emerging from the wall,
as he turns to an exit marked by a red light
he meets her on the stairs.

                         They come together,
fuse, her breast becomes his left chest,
his lower lip rouged, right arm muscular,
the left soft, round and exposed at the shoulder,
right hip shaped like a female's
and on his left foot a black high-heeled pump,
his right leg covered by a half skirt.
Still he is smiling but even more broadly
as in sleep. In the hallway where he stands
transformed people rush by to and from
elevators opening and closing.

He explodes.

■ *Each Day*

Cynthia Matz, with my finger in your cunt
and you sliding back and forth on it,
protesting at the late hour and tiredness
and me with kidneys straining to capacity
with piss I had no chance to release
all night, we got up from the park bench
and walked you home. I left you
at the door. You said something
despairing about taking a chance
and settling on me. I had left Janette
to chase after you running out
of the ice cream parlor where
the three of us had sat—I had felt
so sorry and so guilty to have you
find me with her in the street.
You and I had gone to shows together.
You needed me to talk to and I was glad.
The talk always was about him
whom you still loved. He had jilted
you for someone else. I'm sorry, Cynthia,
that it had to end this way between us too.
I did not return the next day,
after leaving you at the door.
I did not return the following day either.
I went with Janette in whom I felt
nothing standing in the way,
while with you it would have been
each day to listen to your sadness
at having been betrayed by him.
I was not to be trusted either.
I too wanted love pure and simple.

■ *Fingernails*

They look long enough to bite and I attack them
with my teeth, feeling the satisfaction of cutting short
an aggression. I am biting into myself, cutting myself down,
swallowing what I have bitten off to assure its growing back.

I need to cut it down over and over. I am paying
for something wrong but assuring myself of the satisfaction
of seeing that wrong grow back so that I'll have the pleasure
of cutting it down again: sex love: physical love. I fill
my mouth with bitten, sharp fingernails. I could swallow
my whole hand.

■ In the silence we sat across the table
from each other—always there was some obstacle
between us—and bit into our food.
It was our love for one another
disappearing down our throats
never again to emerge
except as waste.

■ *A Moral Tale*

All this for me, he asked,
looking down on her body.
Uh huh, she said, arms stretched out
upon the bed, and she looked up at him
with an amused smile. I think
I'll take it, he said,
and wrapped it up in the sheet
that lay beneath her. He brought
the four ends together in a knot
and slung the body across his back.
He was on his way home to show
his latest find. He had discovered
each body was different
and that altogether they amounted
to a survey of the female form,
something an anthropologist could appreciate,
and he was thinking of becoming one
but there was a hitch: he was bringing
back more bodies than with place
to store them in the house
and it was expensive elsewhere.
He persisted.
He went broke;
his wife left him.
He had to give up his studies;
he had to go back to work
and was left with memories
which to relieve himself in his unhappiness
he would relate at work
where in amazement he was urged to write them down.
The manuscript was published.
The book sold.
There was money again
to return to his studies.

Moral: In adversity we find our goal in life.

■ I give you a little stick, you give me a tiny pebble. We're exciting each other to think differently of ourselves, and we can see an opening in each other that will lead to music and to dance. I probe with the stick, you press with the pebble against my flesh. It hurts, but it's meaningful and we're in love.

■ Once there was a woman smiled at me
from her open door. I wanted her
at once and sat through a political
meeting in her house, thinking
of just this.

■ *At This Moment*

I'm very pleased to be a body. Can there be someone without a body? As you hold mine I feel firmly assured that bodies are the right thing and I think all life is a body. I'm happy about trees, grass and water, especially with the sun shining on it. I slip into it, a summer pleasure.

I have hurt the body. That's when I know I need it most in its whole condition. If I could prove it to you by giving pain you would agree but I prefer you with your body pressed to mine as if to say it is how we know. Think, when two must separate how sad it is for each then having to find another way to affirm their bodies. Knock one against another or tree or rock and there's your pain. Now we have our arms filled with each other. Could we not grow old in this posture and be buried as one body which others would do for us tenderly?

■ *Zoo*

Behind bars
a tiger
moving like striped silk—
a work of art
I want to worship
at its paws.

IV

▪ *Autumn I*

The trees are standing like silent members
of a crowd awaiting decision. They are
rigid and erect, the verdict a foregone
conclusion. I stand before them
guilty but wanting to live—
unsure of myself, timid,
my shoulders hunched.

                       I straighten up
and sing. They remain silent.
I turn around and march off,
working my arms up and down
like a soldier. Having nowhere to go,
nothing in particular to do,
I keep marching.

■ *Autumn II*

For Wendell Berry

A leaf lies shaking
at my door, about to be
blown away.
       If I should
bring it into the still
air of my room, it would
lie quietly on the window sill
facing the tree
from which it fell.

For . . .

Poet of dead farms
dried-up riverbeds and burnt grass
has taken himself to a white room
with barred window to think himself
alive, breathing in, beating his chest
in joy, shouting good tidings
to the trees of his outlook.
What of insanity? For love delivers
him to his foes, praising their hatred
and his guilt. His head hurts,
he is sick to his stomach for coming back
to life in a barred room
the key in his head, love the key:
a dead farm and parched scrub grass.
Abandonment is what he knows.

■ *For John Berryman*

You're dead, what can I do for you?
I am not unsympathetic;
I thought about you often enough
though we never spoke together
but once when I shied away,
feeling something that I fought
in me too—and came out with this
manner of living, by living.

It is depressing to live
but to kill myself in protest
is to assume there is something
to life withheld from me, yet
who withholds it? Think about it.
What is the answer?

But suicide is not so wrong
for one who thought and prayed
his way toward it. I wish, though,
I had known sooner, to have
helped you go on living,
as I do, half a suicide;
the need defended by the other half
that thinks to live in that knowledge
is praiseworthy.

■ *Express Your Will*

Seeing a patch of sky through the trees
I look for a paratrooper
to float down through the leaves
and to beg pardon for his intrusion
and to ask if I enjoy the weather,
sunny and mild. Of course, of course,
I'll answer enthusiastically and he
will unlimber his gun from his shoulder
and fill me with lead.

I thought so, he will say.
I expected you would find the weather good.
Now take a look at me, he will add,
and turn the gun on himself
and pull the trigger. That's to show you
what I really think, he'll say.
But I'll be dead, leaving him for others
to study.

Change, change, change
into a paratrooper.
Make yourself a hunter,
kill,
express your will.

■ *Sh, This Poem Wants to Say Something*

Yes, I was out to visit with my friends
at the bar yesterday when one spoke up
about having a problem. I asked casually
what it could be, with him standing here,
glass in hand, drinking beside me,
and he said, "The problem is me.
I'm wondering what to do with myself
every day, now that there's nothing
to live for except myself."
And I blinked and thought about that
for a while and replied, "That is a problem.
Why not live for me or for your other friends?
How else could we get to meet,
with you gone and then maybe John and Jack
and Jane, each of us taking your position
and doing away with ourselves?" My friend
looked at me for a moment briefly
and asked, "Is that so?"
and we exchanged glances, smiled
and emptied our glasses.

■ In this dream I'm an Indian
confronted by a military commander,
his regiment behind him, seeking
to intimidate me into going away.
I am pointing to earth and sky
to say I am of both
and that it is they who leave
when I go.

        At this, I must wake up
to warn that if what he says is true
all of us are lost. I am the commander's
countryman and in my dream I urge
him to take off his uniform
at once and go bathing
in the nearest spring.

■ In the end is the word to destroy the world
and make a word of it alone
sitting over the water like a cloud
an atomic whitish cloud
like the frost of one's winter breath.
To draw one's breath is to destroy
the world and make a fine haze of it.

■ *For Marianne Moore*

In her garden were flowers
she had not yet named
but they had sprung up
at her consent
and she waited
for the moment
they would become
their colors and their shape
of leaves, for though she saw
them it was not for her
to name them
and to lose their life
in words.

■ I shake my fist at a tree
and say, You will shed your leaves
in time for all your abundance
and variety but I will see to it
that you continue in your present
state in my mind. You have no
memory except in me. I'm
about to write of you
leaf by leaf.

Those dead brown leaves lying at my door
as if to let me see them in their last condition
before they disappear into the fields, I am
your only witness. If I live to have
to see you dead, then there is no answer
to your death but life, and I am living it.

▪ *The Legend of Youth*

In the small square to which we had confined ourselves,
all openings exposed, our fear at a minimum,
finally forgotten, it struck. One of us
rolled upon the ground, the ball locked in his arms.
In the game's excitement he may have tripped;
we could not tell. He did not rise.
There was no sign, nothing had reached out.
We laid him aside and went on,
our glances furtive upon him as we played—
when the next, the ball clasped to his chest,
upright, eyes wide, pitched forward upon his face.
We knew then, and now among the many
in this small square where they lie
in the postures they were caught in,
my back bent far over as a shield,
I sneak a glance
at where the sun stood
and see shadow.

■ *Subway*

I thought that if he could stoop
to pick out rubbish, each piece
placed in his bag—a tedious job
in front of crowds, all day
the trains at a steady roar,
the lighting dim, the air stagnant—
from bin to bin, searching
to the bottom for gum wrappers,
crumpled newspapers, torn sandwich
bags, cigarette stubs, particles
clinging to his fingers. All this
without a word, bending
at the foot of a steel pillar,
it was not too much for me
to be witness.

■ *The Pleasure*

I enjoy watching myself
grow old and gray.
I am authentic, I say,
I belong with the others.

■ When news came of his death I was disappointed.
How many times have I turned away
from silence in a room or among people
and begun to talk into the phone
or nudged a neighbor in a crowd?
I wasn't given brain, tongue, ears, hands,
feet to dwell on silence. I'm sorry
he's dead, and it surely is a disappointment
to him too where he lies, unable to speak
or to move or to make a sign,
so then let us do for him
what he would do for himself, if he could:
ignore this death.

Going Down

There's a hole in the earth I'm afraid of.
I lower myself into it, first tying
one end of a long rope to a tree close by,
the other end around my waist.
I let myself down hand over hand,
gripping the rope hard,
with each step planting my feet
solidly against the sides
that give off an earth odor.

As I descend I breathe less of air
and more a mingling of minerals and clay,
wet, heavy, close. I begin to lose
consciousness and I am afraid
I will loosen my grip on the rope
and fall to the bottom and be suffocated
by dirt chunks falling on top of me
from off the walls. It was this
fear of burial led me to climb down.

■ *In Season*

I have enemies among the leaves.
Listen to the whispering
and the rubbing of bodies
to get close together on the plot.
I'll turn my back
and let them go on with their heated talk
as I await their downfall
in season.

■ *Linguistics*

I heard a man without a tongue talking.
He grunted grammatically.
It was easy to grasp that he wanted a tongue
and was saying he missed it.
I was quite moved and I was delighted
he could signal
but who could help?
What could be done
except to teach him to write
and make that his subject?
We'd embrace him,
knowing that among us were legs,
arms, heads and penises missing
that we could talk about endlessly,
alone.

■ Melpomene in Manhattan

As she walked she would look back
over her shoulder and trip
upon sidewalk cracks or bump
into people to whom she would apologize
profusely, her head still turned.
One could hear her murmur to herself
tearfully, as though filled with a yearning
to recover what she was leaving behind
as if she would preserve it
or do for it what she had neglected
out of ignorance or oversight
or from sheer meanness and spite
or simple helplessness to do better,
her voice beginning to keen
as she tripped or steered blindly
into the gutter
or into hostile crowds.

Their Mouths Full

Let there be ripeness, said the Lord.
And men bowed down to seed brown in the pod
and to its meat palpable and sweet.
And of this fruit you shall eat
for your wisdom, said the Lord.
And of none other, lest you die.
And the men ate of the ripened fruit
and rejoiced in its taste
and of the seed split between their teeth,
for these too were sweet of their kind;
and so it happened that unripened fruit
was looked on with scorn
and beaten down from its branches
in the Lord's name as sinful
and the work of death.
And men sat themselves down to grow
palpable and sweet to one another
in the sun and it was then time to die,
ripening, and they died,
blessing their maker,
their mouths full of one another.

■ Prose Poem in Six Parts

I

I'm so happy, he shouts, as he puts a bullet through his head. It leaves a clean hole on either side of the skull, no blood pouring out. I'm so happy, he shouts at his triumph. He knew it would happen this way, pulling the trigger. He knew it, he had imagined it and he collapses of a spasm of joy.

His friends look closely at the clean hole on either side and decide to take their own thoughts seriously too and act. It will not be with a pistol but with each other whom they have had on their minds for so long without daring to speak openly about it. They speak and become trans-fixed in each other's image. They are not exactly dead, they are unmoving but fulfilled. They are not even aware of being happy or depressed and the way domestic animals roam among them nibbling at their fingers, ears, toes and nose is how these animals eat at flowers and grass. To the transfixed it is a happy identification. They can believe the world is whole, all this without saying a word, their eyes starry.

2

Their eyes starry, their bodies glistening with sweat that acts like a lacquer to seal their pores, they grow rigid, gleam like polished stone. They can recall the one who put a bullet through his head. He has risen and walks among them tapping on each body for a response to his happiness, each tap like his heartbeat to inform each rigid body exhibiting its own happiness. These are mutually dependent acts but tapping his way from body to body, his imagination proven to him, he is not aware of their happiness while the one person who is aware of this di-lemma has not yet shot himself in the head or talked to another human about each other. He could be lonely were it not for the sight of these who are so happy in themselves. They promise much and he has a relative hope for the future.

3

He has a relative hope for the future. He lights up a cigar and observes the community of polished stones and the one pierced skull and wishes to make himself totally familiar with their lives. He examines the clean hole in the head. He treats himself to a glass of wine. He has doubts, he finds it hard to discover their sources. By examining himself in the mirror he can see his mood. By turning his face from the mirror he can see the bath. By turning from the bath he can see the towel rack. By turning from the towel rack he can see the toilet bowl. By turning from the toilet bowl he has made a complete circle and is back staring into the mirror. It's somebody about whom he has doubts, he has discovered in one complete revolution. By marching out of the bathroom he will leave the image behind him in the mirror and by leaving it behind he is free. Who is he now? He has doubts.

4

He has doubts. He chews upon the stump of his cigar. He can express himself but to what end? Language is not the solution. He can join the rigid aggregate community but in what posture? He could make love to himself but with what thoughts? He could warm himself by the fire in winter, cool himself in the sea in summer. He could eat when hungry. He could cry when in pain, he could laugh when amused, he could think when in trouble. He is an ordinary man.

5

He is an ordinary man, he wants his breakfast, he needs his unhappiness, he wishes to be himself, he desires apotheosis as he is and so he shoots himself to relieve himself of his doubts. Brought to consciousness by this act, he dies. The man with the clean hole through his skull does not know the ordinary man is dead and the aggregate community never cares to change from its transfixed postures while he, lying dead, is studying that compelling emptiness in him beneath his breastbone and does not know how either to fill it or extract it to give him peace. He yearns to leap up from the floor to become a whirling dancer, an ecstatic, for the hell of it.

6

For the hell of it he tries but lies still. He then knows he is dead and would inform the world. His body will, he decides. It is the evidence and his silence the message, and now what does life have to offer? It is time to think. He thinks, the earth has the answer that it presses upon him where he lies. Not to think is the answer. He can be a stone or a cycle of existence, inside the cycle the air of emptiness, a small hole for a small life such as he had seen in the skull of the risen one. He can be a stone with a hole in it and he will always be the same. He has his comfort, he is ready to die successfully, he dies and is complete, an ordinary man.

■ When I see fish swimming in schools
I ask if I may join, I'm very sad
that we must stay apart
in this only world we have
between us. I see looks exchanged
among men and women, lips to bodies,
and when they part, I think
I am surrounded by a loud wailing
in the air. I raise my voice
in grief too, my one identity
with others.

Tread the Dark

For Stanley Kunitz

I am writing
upon the expanding wall
of the cosmos.

■ *1. Brightness as a Poignant Light*

I tread the dark and my steps are silent.
I am alone and feel a ghostly joy—wildly
free and yet I do not live absolutely
and forever, but my ghostly joy
is that I am come to light
for some reason known only to the dark,
perhaps to view itself in me.

As I tread the dark,
led by the light of my pulsating mind,
I am faithful to myself: my child.
Still, how can I be happy
to have been born only to return
to my father, the dark, to feel his power
and die?

I take comfort that I am
my father, speaking as a child
against my fatherhood. This
is the silence I hear my heart
beating in, but
not for me.

■ 2. From the Observatory

Each step is to and from an object
and does not echo in heaven
or in hell. The earth vibrates
under the heel or from impact
of a stone. Many stones fall
from outer space and earth itself
is in flight. It heads out
among the stars that are dead,
dying or afire.

■ 3.

The seasons doubt themselves and give way
to one another. The day is doubtful of itself,
as is the night; they come, look around, slowly depart.
The sun will never be the same.
People give birth to people, flourish
and then die
and the sun is a flame of doubt
warming to our bodies.

4. With the Sun's Fire

Are you a horror to yourself?
Do you have eyes peering at you
from within at the back of your skull
as you manage to stay calm, knowing
you are being watched by a stranger?

Be well, I am seated beside you,
planning a day's work. We are contending
with the stuff of stones and stars,
with water, air, with dirt, with food
and with the sun's fire.

■ 5.

Examine me, I am continuous
from my first memory and have no memory
of birth. Therefore was I never born
and always have been? As told
in my breathing which is never new
or tired?

       Face in the mirror
or star hidden by the sun's rays,
you are always there but which am I
and who is the mirror or the hidden star?
Explain me as you are that I may live
in time and die
when I am dead.

■ 6. The Two Selves

I existed before my mind realized me
and when I became known to myself
it was with the affection for warmth
beside a radiator.

   So you began for me
and I will whisper to your self
to give in, to surrender, to close
in remembrance, and I will give you up
and withdraw into a stone, forever
known to you.

■ 7. The Juggler

He bows and extracts from his pockets a live rabbit, a
tiger cub, a rooster, a monkey, a musical instrument. Is it
an oboe? And he is ready and heaves all into the air with
one heave and quickly catches each on its way down, then
sends them up again, singly this time, one after the other.
They squawk, hiss, growl, chatter, crow. The oboe emits
music! In protest? Who can tell? It is music and that's all.
And the juggler is laughing, laughing like a clown and
nobody wonders why he uses live things.

■ 8. Scenario

An old man realizes that he is seeing signs of a bodily reversion to his youth. His skin appears fresh and smooth around the thighs where it had been wrinkled and flabby; his white hair shows streaks of the original black, his sagging chin line is gone. One morning, he confronts the startling image of himself in his twenties. It frightens him and exhilarates him also, and he goes rushing to show himself to his wife who looks at him and begins to weep.

He grows younger still and leaves his wife and finds himself a young woman to live with. Life is merry again, and he grows younger still, and his new wife begins to laugh at him. He has regressed to his teens, mind and body reverting to an excitable, incoherent stage. He grows even younger, becomes a lisping child, becomes an infant, then a squalling newborn. He returns to fetus stage. He loses all sense of himself and his surroundings. He becomes an ovum. For all practical purposes, he no longer exists, but when he begins to sense himself again it's as he emerges from a wet, pulsating warm cleft with the help of a pair of forceps around his throbbing head.

■ 9.

There's the reality: a truck passes by on the road outside my window. I have my knees crossed on the couch looking up at the trees and listening to the birds, as if I believed they had reality licked by being just birds utterly content with themselves. I could say the same for the truck but as for myself, aware of the truck, the trees and myself, my mind is restless and seeking to replace the real with its own version—also to be reckoned with.

I agree, I want the truck to pass by my house, I want the birds to sing, I want the trees to rest upon themselves, I want my knees crossed upon the couch. I want to call all this the reality. And I must settle for a question.

■ 10.

Paint a wall
cover the weather stains
and spider webs: who's happy

You who don't exist
I make you
out of my great need
There is no prose for this
no ordered syntax
no carefully measured tread
I am falling beyond depth
into oblivion
breathing
I hear breathing
Something must be said
of nothing

I am as queer as the conception of God
I am the god and the heaven
unless I scatter myself
among the animals and furniture of earth

■ *II.*

Holes I want to creep into
and pull the cover over me
darken my mind.
I'll learn how it feels
to feel nothing.

I have a glowing heart
in an empty space.
I lie down beside it
and warm myself.

12. An Account in the Present Tense of How It All Happened

I am about to close the refrigerator after removing a package of meat when I hear my door lock turning and a crew of men, without so much as first knocking, walk in. They stride directly over to the refrigerator, tie rope around it, hoist it upon a dolly and ride it out the door. Who are these people and why are they taking my refrigerator when there is nothing wrong with it? They are making some kind of mistake. Stop, I cry. You are in the wrong apartment. Not one turns his head to look at me or to listen. At that moment, three men, a second crew almost on the heels of the first, stride in and lift up my television set between them and walk out with it. I scream for help. I pound their shoulders but get no response, as if they were made of wood. I scream and scream, and another crew is right behind the second, this time to remove my bed. I am going to be left with nothing, nothing. I am about to get on the phone to call the police when I notice that they have cut the wires and taken the phone with them.

They remove dishes, cutlery, rugs, books, lamps; screw out the bulbs. They leave me an empty apartment and begin to tear down the apartment walls. They knock out the walls of the building itself. I flee into the street, just barely in time before they begin to attack the stairs and the elevator. Out in the street I see that it's happening to each apartment building on the block. All the tenants are milling around, with the few clothes on their backs they managed to grab and are shouting at each other in panic and wild rage. We are totally stranded; there are no police and no emergency crews in sight. The streets are beginning to resemble a bombed-out area, and we see that we will have to fend for ourselves with our bare hands. There is a park nearby, and we begin to converge upon it. It has large, open spaces where we will be able to lie down and rest and perhaps make our beds there for the night with what linen and bedclothes we were able to rescue from inhuman hands. It's all over, it seems, that which gave us our comforts and pleasures. It's back to the woods and fields. Did anybody bring a knife or a gun with which to hunt a rabbit or a bird? We look at each other, beginning to understand.

■ 13. At the End of the World

Emanuel puffed at his cigar as he studied the monster, twenty stories high. Emanuel, standing at its feet, each the length, breadth and height of a pyramid, looked up and down at the figure. Then as it began to bend—what a roar its movement made, like an approaching hurricane—to pick him up in its hands, each the length, breadth and bulk of a whale, Emanuel removed the cigar from his mouth and from his pocket which held a penknife that he used for peeling apples—pulled out the knife, flipped open the blade and cut his throat.

14.

It's midnight, the house is silent.
In the distance a musical instrument
is being played softly. I am alone,
and it's as if the world has come to an end
on a low, musical note.

15.

The sky makes no sense to me.
What is it saying? Blue? That blue is enough?
The blue of emptiness?

A small cloud trails beneath the sky
as if to make a point
about its pride in being a body,
white, welcome to the eye.

The cloud drifts out of sight.
In its absence, I will walk
beneath the sky, slowly drifting
in and out of streets and bars.

■ *16.*

I am standing on the soft, spongy surface of my brain and looking down into the space between the halves, expecting the surface to give way under my weight and hurl me down. The surface caves in suddenly and I fall. I am an object in space flying downward, head over heels, shrieking my terror though I am falling without harm to me physically, but lost, lost without foothold, without hope of foothold. I have done this to myself, I say as I fall, and since this is what I did in all consciousness, then I cannot blame myself either. It could not save me, it is no rescue, and I accept myself falling and sing out my terror like a song.

■ *17. The Procession*

It is a man held aloft on a spit
and carried over the heads of the crowd
chanting its terror and acceptance.
One of them is next.
When a corpse begins to smell
there will be a fresh one
to keep the rest remindful
of the price of peace.

■ *18.*

The trouble is that I can't occupy
the emptiness around me
while everyone looks at me
as if my desire to fill this vacuum
is some sort of madness or foolish whim.
Their eyes wide and motionless,
I fill my time walking
with hunched shoulders
in a crowd of silent faces.

■ *19.*

I wake up from a slime pit,
an unfinished man in the ages
of the flower-eating monsters:
it was the sadness of animals
who tracked their way along the given
road of their existence to its predicted end,
sprawled on their side in the snow
or in a ditch, partly eaten by another.

I missed love and tenderness on awakening
and said to myself silently,
Why am I like other creatures
when I feel myself invincible?
Am I a fool to think?

20. *The Abandoned Animal*

There was an animal whose keeper had died;
the food left in the cage was plentiful,
but excrement covered the floor.
In winter he could pad upon it firmly
enough but in summer heat sank
to his joints. There was danger,
though, his body mounted on the rising waste,
the ceiling drawing close, his neck
stretched forward to give him room.

It made the poor animal whine,
to have to be crushed by his own appetite,
and at each mouthful
he could not think of its pleasure
without wanting to die.

■ *21.*

I have found what I want to do—
to kill myself quietly
I can do it slowly
in my sleep
or nourish it
in me at my work—
jealous of those
who have died
because life's needs
were endless but death
was satisfied with little.

■ *22. This False Desire*

This false desire for life as I enjoy the sight of leaves turn-
ing brown, red, orange against the clear blue sky. The
leaves wave in the wind to urge me to falsehood, to make
myself a chanter of life, a bard who calls on others to live
for the glory of living. I'm tempted but I refuse. I think
death has its pleasures that I surmise from the dead who
lie very still, strictly attentive to each syllable and motion
of their death as it attends on them, stretched out like
children under the hypnotic crooning of the mother.

23.

Inside me is the peace of an egg,
round and smooth to myself,
white as a beginning.
Outside my window snow is falling
on the sagging garden shack,
so peaceful too under snow.

Peace of the snow, silence and stillness
where no figure treads.
This is a warm death
under a snow roof.
I want to live amid silence and falling snow.
I want the snow to believe me
and fall peacefully until I fall
from my place in spirals like a flake.

I hear blackbirds breaking the silence.
Keep the newspapers out of the house
and take the phone off the hook
and let the mail rot in the mailbox.
I can't take disturbance, I love the snow.
My life is happier under snow,
I nestle in my own warmth.

It will be days before another human being approaches,
the drifts are too high around the house.
Snow without fault.
I am prepared to enjoy it.

■ 24.

Cautiously, to die cautiously
into the wind would be a way
known in a dream
and I walk into the wind
head down dreaming this wind
is the way
and I seeking to enter.

25. A Recounting

I sat among the dead and heard their insides
rot and fall apart with a sigh
as it were the sound made by the dying.
In the night in the silence
amidst the cricket whirr on all sides
I heard the tearing sighs and it was like
complaining talk that it was better
to be alive, young especially, when each muscle
was firm and the body sprang.

I listened and heard more
but it was the same said in different sounds
of breaking and falling apart
and it was difficult to leave
for I felt that all being said here
I would say among the living and to say it
was to be futile and repetitious
and so I decided it was time, rather, to dance,
to silence their sighs by my listening
to the rhythm of my steps and I found
I had danced my way out of their midst
and upon a highway empty and stretching far off
into the distance, my blood warm, my heartbeat
fast. I danced and I danced, now a tango,
now a waltz but always a reaching out
with my legs to a deliberate passion
to meet the will I had called up face to face
to be at one with myself
to give birth to myself whole
whom I could love so that love ruled me.

I danced and the rabbits of the field came
to the edge of the road to watch
and to run across my path as a test
that I was not there to kill. They were
making little of my ecstasy and I began

to walk, throwing weary glances behind me
until I tired and sat upon a rock
at the roadside and counted the ants
busying themselves around a stone
where there were holes they disappeared into
with tiny sticks and leaves between their mandibles
for building a house or a palace down below.
I had nothing to do and nowhere to go
but it was time to move to find something
to forget myself. I had danced, I had walked,
I had more yet to do before dying
when I would know that it too
was but another state of things.
I saw traffic beginning, the sun up,
and I thumbed my way back
to an angry, clamorous city.

26. Dante's Brother

There's my tiger standing in the woods. He and I belong together. If he's hungry he'll eat me, if he can catch me. I've killed when hungry and I've ordered animals killed when others could do it better and quicker, and I have looked at the same animals alive with curiosity and made up stories about them for my amusement and to explain to myself our relationship to one another. My tiger stands perfectly still, as if he were thinking of the mystery of others too and seeking for an explanation.

■ *27.*

I hold a pair of scissors over my head and open and close the blades to cut off the air from its source. I lower the scissors to the ground and snap at the surface to punish it for its errors, such as grass, trees, flowers and fruit. I turn the scissors' point toward myself, snap the blades open and shut at my nose, my eyes, my mouth, my ears. I have to be angry at myself also who lives off earth and air.

Why is there hurt and sorrow? Scissors, cut them off from me. Scissors, whose fine steel gleams in the sunlight like a most joyful smile, why am I not like you instead, since I must give pain? I do not want to feel it in others. I do not want to feel it in myself. I do not want to be a man cutting through grass and flesh in the sunlight.

■ *28.*

I am dreaming of the funeral of the world, watching it go by carried in an urn, reduced to ashes, and followed by a horde of mourners, a million abreast, across the broadest lands and all chanting together, We are dead, we have killed ourselves. We are beyond rescue. What you see is not us but your thoughts of us, and I who am observing in terror of it being true hope not to have to wake up, so that I may let myself discount it as a dream.

29. Apocrypha

People came to watch him
chew on steak or pear
and spit it out. He
sat cross-legged or moved about
silently, shaking hands
mildly or patting a shoulder,
speaking always in low, pleasant tones.

What was to be made of this man
who did not eat, drink or defecate
in the world? He seemed
to want only to taste its fruits
and let them go, happy
that the world had so many
wonderful flavors. It was this
that irritated observers, and many
hated him, after secretly trying
his way, and starving, shrunk
to skin and bones. It proved
to them he was not human,
and so he died.

■ 30. *The Suicide*

I find I have opened a vein in warm water and watch with curiosity dark red flow over the surface in long wavery patterns beautiful to see. Soon the surface will be covered and already I am drowsy, wondering how to stop the flow. My arms are too weak to raise me from the tub and if I do not do something quickly I'm going to die.

I am not curious about death, its absolute silence. I shall not be able to appreciate the beautiful wavery patterns of my blood. Now I cannot even call for help. I resign myself to having done what I did so that I may die at peace with myself, peace at last as I have not had in life, pushing myself to be other than what I was. I was a man who loved his ease and his thoughts and who wished only to stare out the window, but, knowing that he had to act to be acknowledged as a man, I have acted.

■ 31. The Dead Sea

It is so still that tracks have been laid
on piles driven into the bottom; and now
people ride their trains, occasionally curious
as to the origin of this sudden collapse
of the sea, but take it as a good omen
for traveling and communication. No wild winds,
no tall waves that ships especially designed for
had learned to climb, trained seamen
in command: a universe of dread abandoned.

One man states having patted the snout
of the once fierce meat-eating shark;
it exposed its teeth in a grin,
and now cameras daily ride the trains;
and it has been rumored the water turns
to glass when eyes are averted—an amazement
to travelers who now move quickly
and peacefully to and from business.
One man, it has been verified, dived off
the first trestle crossing and has not come up
since, in company of the fish,
swimming among them. Reading about it,
the people shuddered.

■ 32. *Theme and Variations*

How do you get to scream the world is good
and we have only to lose ourselves in its goodness?
Ask me in return and together we'll question
each man, woman and child we meet,
and won't it be the Lord's Prayer
if we all get up on our feet and shout
out the question rhythmically
because it is a passion
to know.
                    .

You sit drinking milk
knowing your faults,
milk drinking
your last gesture
to childhood.
                    .

Look at my smooth face
cover my failings.
I smile, I add
to the picture of health.
                    .

You strike me
and I'll strike you
and when we are through
beating each other
nearly dead, about to die,
we will be close
to an understanding of ourselves
as wanting to die
in the quickest, most efficient way
without sacrificing pleasure
as a principle of life.
                    .

There's love in me like an egg hardened.
What do you think would have emerged
if it had been kept warm
and allowed to hatch?

I am an affectionate man,
I love the differences
that compose me.

■ *33.*

I am going to where nobody else can be heard
talking, so wide and lonely a place
that when I talk it will be to myself,
puzzled by it, judging a stranger,
pronouncing good or evil because it is necessary
to know which for my own, the speaker's,
commitment to his place. It will echo
him, will make him listen to himself,
to suffer the fool gladly.
I am going off into the hardness
we reserve for ourselves.

■ 34. Suicide in Two Voices

Shit on this world.
What did I say?
Shit on this world.
I don't have any compliments for it either. I
    couldn't care less.
Oh fuck you too for being shocked.
I'm not shocked.
Even Beethoven sounds genteel and romantic,
    crying to his soul.
I'm giving him the door. I'm not being whimsical.
Get the hell out of here.
I'm angry.
I'm a god-damn human being.
Hey, man, do you like what I'm doing here?
Who cares if you don't, you human being.
Go shoot more of your own kind.
What are you hanging around here for,
    listening to me shoot off my mouth.
Go, go to hell.
I shit on all of you, the living and the dead.
Sue me.
You rapist pig.
You're only happy when you kill.
Well, so I am, killing you off with this. And
    now I'm all alone,
as far as I'm concerned, and I'll put this
    poem through my skull.

■ *35.*

I say hello to the grass, it stays silent. I say hello to the ground, hello to the trees. I say hello to myself—"But you I know, I need an answer from the others."

I should plant trees and grass in my mind, pour earth into my thinking. It works, I grow silent, too. I do not know my life from theirs.

■ *36. Death of a Lawn Mower*

It died in its sleep,
dreaming of grass,
its knives silent and still,
dreaming too, its handlebars
a stern, abbreviated cross
in tall weeds. Where is he
whom it served so well?
Its work has come to nothing,
the dead keep to themselves.

■ 37. Is There a Value to Life?

Four squares, two below, two placed on top, combine to form a new and larger square. A fifth makes for a problem. It either should be removed or broken up and distributed among the others or placed as a sort of cap or peak. It could be kept moving over the surface of the four squares and stopped only at those particular parts that seem congruent with it at that moment. It could be made to wander as a kind of roving observer or explorer over every side. It could be placed at the very center of these four squares spread apart, with an edge of each resting on an edge of the centered fifth square.

Finding these suggestions unsatisfactory, why not mold all five into a ball? But that would eliminate their identity. Then suppose we mark off on the surface of this ball an area which each theoretically occupies, labeling each area One, Two, Three, Four and Five respectively. Would that be fair? In a way, yes. Still, none would remain intact in its original shape and so the problem of identity would not be solved.

Well, is identity necessary? I'm relieved to think about that openly.

■ *38. Cannibals*

I bite off a strip of my own flesh
hanging from a red wound
and it tastes sour. God,
I am startled; no, shocked—
I must admit, and I think
of cannibals. Why would they
want to eat people at all,
once tasting their flesh?
I spit out my piece,
rejecting my body, my life,
feeling guilty and ashamed.

■ *39. The Sportsman*

Shutting out the cries of the dying and hungry, the im-
prisoned and the tortured, beginning life all over again
in innocence under the sun in sweat and energy for myself
as a person, to celebrate myself once again and for always,
now that I know the worst, that I must die in any case, I
am on the handball court, shouting and playing my way
through the miseries of others, making myself a figure of
the beautiful life.

Players join me in the game and when we smile at each
other we are sharing the secret, and when one of us wins,
both panting from exertion, the winner is courteous and
deferential so that the loser may reconcile himself in good
spirits.

■ 40. *South Bronx*

Where am I in all this? Under a heap of rubble some-where in the middle, awaiting the nose of the rat to sniff me out and to think a moment of my human smell. The rat will find it hard to understand, back off, bare its teeth, turn tail and run. But I am nothing at all. I am refuse. I am a junked body. I cannot be repaired. I have damaged irreplaceable parts, eyes that refuse to see any longer, turned in on themselves, arms that stick to my sides, un-able and unwilling to move, out of a lack of anything for them to do, legs stiff and straight out before me, never having had anywhere to go, never put to use to walk the world. My stomach is shrunken and beyond food because what I was served as food never really fed me. But I could be useful. I am garbage like any battered open can or empty milk carton. I want at least to be found useful by the rat to regain pride in myself before I moulder into insensibility. If he hates and fears me then it's because it was my species that hunted him at one time and forced him to eat garbage in secret humiliation. He is confusing me with my own kind—if only he would understand, and I could help by becoming unrecognizable, a pulp of flesh.

■ 41. *The Forest Warden*

I notice the earth is not shaken by this fire
though it lies blackened and silent. I notice too
that the air is floating seed pods down onto the ground
beneath the ash from which they should emerge
in time as tiny shoots. Nothing would spring from me.

Another man would have to take my place
at the table and walk through the dead forest
searching for life, if he were curious and full of pity.
I would die neutrally.

I was happy for a while
which said something for the usefulness in being born.
I have been sad much longer and in doubt
which also speaks of a purpose, hidden from me or lost.
I say let this fire burn and let this man that I am
die in the fire or try to save himself.
Whatever I do is a fire.

■ 42. The Only One I Know

The leaves turn and twist in the wind
as if quarreling with one another
and with themselves. Several fly off
to their death upon the ground
where they are carried along
like torn dollar bills.
The wind has enclosed my head in its pressure.
How nice it would be
to tumble along the ground,
all my living hopes for my own kind
disproven anyway.

                      We move around each other,
we are not harmful. We are events,
right as volcanoes.

Black trees, the irreducible pain
of the missing happiness, forgetfulness gone,
finish of pleasure. Buildings stand,
raised by an effort, himself needing his own will
to remain upright. "Unknown cause, existence of my body,
I go with you only because I feel you and I are one,
the only one I know."

I am plastering myself into the wall of an apartment house. I want to be secure against any further wandering or abuse of myself. As part of the wall of a new apartment house, I can rest assured of serving the cause of shelter and other humane considerations. It will be a pleasure to listen to the sounds of music and talk piercing the wall on a pleasant night or day. I also can listen in on some heavy problems and, of course, those intimate pleasures reserved only for couples in the privacy of their bedrooms. Am I plastering myself into the wall for that purpose, really? Then I will live a long and exciting life, simply by standing upright.

Now I wonder whether I should invite a companion to stay with me, a woman I could trust who would enjoy my pleasures and approve. Together we could listen in on others while ourselves remain secreted. I hurry the job of plastering myself in, not waiting to call or write to the woman of my choice. She will know easily enough, I believe, what I want of her when she hears what I have done and will simply do the same, a few bricks above or below me. It really doesn't matter. I'm indifferent as to where, just so long as we stand together in the same wall.

■ 44. *The Life They Lead*

I wonder whether two trees standing side by side really need each other. How then did they spring up so close together? Look how their branches touch and sway in each other's path. Notice how at the very top, though, they keep the space between them clear, which is to say that each still does its thinking but there is the sun that warms them together.

Do their roots entangle down there? Do they compete for nourishment in that fixed space they have to share between them, and if so, is it reflected in their stance toward one another, both standing straight and tall, touching only with their branches. Neither tree leans toward or away from the other. It could be a social device to keep decorum between them in public. Perhaps their culture requires it and perhaps also this touching of branches to further deceive their friends and associates as to the relationship between them—while what goes on beneath the surface is dreadful, indeed, roots gnarled and twisted or cut off from their source by the other and shrunken into lifelessness, with new roots flung out desperately in a direction from the entanglement, seeking their own private, independent sources. As these two trees stand together, they present to the eye a picture of benign harmony, and that may be so, with both dedicated to the life they lead.

■ *45.*

Smash myself against a wall
to feel how deeply I love life
in protest at the silence
in routine work to keep a house.
Silent house, its anguish stilled
in bed under covers in the night
of no history and no memory.
Night without appetite,
zero night, ringing ears listening
to silence of no future. Night
of fixation on death, seeking it
like sex, pursuing it awake
and in dreams and token deeds
to bring it on—and then the laughter
of a Pepsi-Cola kid outside
who howls his adolescence,
smashes the bottle against the curb.
I laugh. He is in my company,
with the first smashed bottle.

■ 46. A Meditation

There's no gunpowder for my gun
I want to shoot a lion
I want to put on a lion's skin
I want to be a man
I want to kill myself bravely
as a lion   I want to be joyous
I want to live   I want love
I want myself

I want to be born again
I want everything
I do not want sadness
I do not want myself
I do not want pleasure
I do not want happiness
I want sacrifice
I want to sacrifice myself
I want to be God's confidant and right hand
I want mercy and pity and love and gentleness
and warmth and honor and blessing and victory
over my sadness
I'm a lion
with a gentle face
and I can be killed with ease
I am you, best friend
Why am I so sad

I am filled with promise
I exude confidence
I am a grave
I want to be obvious about it
filled with its own dirt
There's nothing you can tell me
or do that could move me
I am waiting at the end of the world

I am somebody you know
We never met

■ *47.*

I placed myself inside an iron cage and threw away the key to experience being trapped, but now someone appears and thinks this actually is what I want. I have been standing silently, gripping the bars through morning, noon and night, as he notices, on his way to and from house or work, and his curiosity is no longer aroused. I can't ask him to find the key, because he will then realize that I am imprisoned unwillingly and become suspicious and call up the police. I am in a vulnerable position, of my own doing.

Well, I will live out this entrapment as best I can, with dignity and smiles to all who come upon me so that they think I am perfectly happy in my role. Oh, I can expect admiration and applause, interviews in the public press. I shall have to affirm my willingness to be entrapped and learn how to enjoy the wonder it will arouse among my witnesses.

■ 48. At the Museum

This wax figure against a wall moving
arms, legs, head at a push of a button
in its palm and with label reading, Official Version,
pinned to a lapel, resembled me.
I looked around, frightened
and began to walk off as casually as I could,
turning my face from those coming in
to push the button. It talked.
I heard my voice saying I was well
and thank you and how are you
and good to see you and let's meet again—
everything I'd say in everyday exchange
in and out of office hours—
this very same figure inviting a colleague
home for dinner, with wife waiting
graciously at the door, and this invited person—
but it was another wax figure;
I saw its eyes staring ahead
until my form reached over and pressed
the button in the guest's palm.
I ran. I am home now.
I waste time. I lie around.
I drink sodas, I think a lot.
I shall not leave this house again.
I have been made useless,
I can be thrown away.

■ 49. The Question

I dream I am flying above the city
on the strength of my two outflung arms
and looking down upon the streets
where people are like so many
bacteria moving about upon a slide.
I am alone up here, with no one
to contradict me, free of the noise,
tumult and violence of the living.
Here is my true residence,
and if I say the people are bacteria
who will deny it? I declare
in my circumstances that the people
are what I say they are. The only
question now is whether I can
keep flying.

■ *50.*

I'm afraid to open the door,
something will come at me,
I'll scream and want to die
quickly in its grasp.

I'm afraid to open the door
to see myself behind it
with mouth crushed open
trying to stand up straight.

I'm afraid to open the door
to what I've been evading,
my guilt at others loving me,
devious and a liar, myself
in a coat of shit behind the door.

But what if I am standing there
behind it smiling at my fears,
my arms embracing me?
I'm afraid to open the door.

■ *51.*

I sink back upon the ground, expecting to die. A voice speaks out of my ear, You are not going to die, you are being changed into a zebra. You will have black and white stripes up and down your back and you will love people as you do not now. That is why you will be changed into a zebra that people will tame and exhibit in a zoo. You will be a favorite among children and you will love the children in return whom you do not love now. Zoo keepers will make a pet of you because of your round, sad eyes and musical bray, and you will love your keeper as you do not now. All is well, then, I tell myself silently, listening to the voice in my ear speak to me of my future. And what will happen to you, voice in my ear, I ask silently, and the answer comes at once: I will be your gentle, musical bray that will help you as a zebra all your days. I will mediate between the world and you, and I will learn to love you as a zebra whom I did not love as a human being.

■ *52.*

I'm alone and none of my furniture
comes forward to comfort me: the desk
stands silent against the wall; the bookcase
will not move from its corner; the filing
cabinet is fixed in its place. I am
alone among the world's goods such as they are,
but who will get them to speak to me
or to act in their own behalf, dumb things
that they are, with no sense of themselves
or of others, and so I grieve,
my loneliness filled with their presence:
I exist.

■ *53. The Vase*

See how tall and straight I stand
with blossoms above me. Could anything
be more beautiful than I who am nothing
but an enclosure upon emptiness?

■ 54.

If trees which have the best life of all,
belonging in one place and never moving
yet always renewing themselves,
if they don't complain when they must die
why should I, who have a far more restless
existence? I should be glad
to die into some permanent place
in the earth, and because I am not glad
and seek after the life of the trees,
I remain fixed in my own unhappiness
which is a place I cannot leave
wherever I go on earth in search
of peace, and since I have a kind of permanence
in which I should content myself
I am identified with trees.

■ *55. The Metamorphosis*

Bumping against rock in the dark,
he becomes the rock, stiffening in pain.
The pain fades and he becomes the lightness
and relief. He moves
and becomes the movement.
A rock is in his path once more;
he falls to his knees
in awe of his past self.

His knees make him a suppliant
of his changes. He seeks to know
and becomes a form of the curious.
He touches himself at all points
and becomes his hands.
They touch stone,
a change he remembers,
and he becomes the remembrance
and moves nimbly in the dark
from rock to rock.

56. The Explorer

I have this mountain to climb
and no one to stop me,
this dangerous mountain
of glaciers and gaunt cliffs,
and I will climb it
for the sake of the living.
Climb, then, they call out,
and die. Climb, then, I answer,
softly, and live. I am
about to begin.

I am reaching for possession.
Climb, then, they whisper, and live.

My joy is in the trees and grass,
the rocks and glacial face
of the mountain. My joy is skyward,
my life is the opening of heaven.
I have placed my foot on the mountain
that I have discovered is my own.

■ 57. *In My Dream*

I've made an order for myself and it is through its tightly fitted parts that the child returns. He keeps sneaking back and running gleefully from one statue to the next, smearing each with crayons and muddy fingers. As I chase after him to drive him out, he hides behind my great, stone monoliths. He can dash from statue to statue before I even start to run. He holds in his hand a doll that squeaks when he squeezes it. He fondles it and croons to it that it belongs to him. It's all his; he will let no one touch it, and he sticks out his tongue at me as I reach to grab the doll from him so that he might grow up and become as I am, stolid, stoic, enduring.

He escapes me with his squeaking doll, and I begin to see the humor of it. I'm sorry for him trying to return after I excluded him. He must see something to want to come back, so now I let him play around with my most valued art: the statue of respectability, that of congeniality, that of cooperativeness, of the concerned citizen and many, many others that I wander among in admiration of my sculptural talent, living among the evidence, eating my bread at their feet and making my bed against the gallery wall, becoming in sleep the figure of peacefulness and fulfillment. The child tickles me on the nose as I sleep, and I rub my nose sleepily, knowing dimly in the back of my mind that it is he teasing me. I don't mind; he loves me with all my self-satisfactions. He needs me, apparently. He needs someone to play with; he will play with me in these circumstances, and I tell myself, Why not, he gives me affection. All my statues are silent. When I speak he mimics me. When I raise my hand to begin a new work he mocks me with his doll that he pretends to shape with his finger and with solemn face. I shall be making new statues of all kinds: to goodness, to contentment, to pleasure, to happiness and so on but each now will have the child's influence, just that touch of humor by which I will be separated from the thing itself, and the child and I will enjoy ourselves together, and the old silence within me that made me uncomfortable and drove me to forget myself in work will have vanished in laughter between us.

■ *58.*

Did you know that hair is flying around in the universe? Hair trimmed from beards in barbershops, from mustaches at the mirror, from underarms, from crotches, legs and chests—human hair. It all gets dumped into a fill-in space and then the wind gets at it and sails it back into the cities and towns and villages, right through your open windows during summer and even during winter down your chimney. Hair, brown, black, red, white, grey and yellow. They get all mixed up and you find them on your pullover sweater and wonder who did you come up against with yellow hair which you happen to like and you dream of its actually having happened that you were in touch with a person with yellow hair.

That's not the whole of it. Think of walking through the street on a windy day or even on a calm, balmy day. The hair is floating all around you and you are walking through perhaps an invisible or fine mist of cut hairs. Black, brown, red that you would not have cared to touch in a million years because you associate them with certain kinds of faces and behavior but there are the hairs of these people touching and clinging to you, as if trying to tell you that hair is everywhere and everybody has it and that it's hopeless to try to pick black or brown or red off your sleeves but not yellow hair.

It would be an act of insanity. You need to pick them all off or none and let yourself be covered by them all, like a new kind of fur coat or perhaps a new hairy skin to protect you from the weather. Hair of all colors. What a pretty sight that would make, wouldn't it, and you would have a coat of many colors, and I bet you would be proud of it, especially if you saw everyone else wearing a coat of many colors. How about that? Because people cut their hair and let it fly out over the world where it lands on everyone and everyone is sharing in the coat of many colors.

■ *59.*

To Charles Reznikoff

I think I am being swirled like a leaf
and I think there is wisdom
in letting myself go
and looking with a careful eye
for a landing place or a calm shoal
of wind. I say this because
I do not think it is a wind
that can be resisted
without being torn apart
and I am not mistaken;
this is the faith
I must have,
not to think life and death
synonymous.

60. *The Pleasure*

When I watch myself
grow old and grey,
I am authentic, I say.
I belong with the others.

Body, listen to me:
we don't have long to live
together but when you have
crumbled into dust
stir yourselves
when the wind blows
and fly.

61.

Standing by the sea I hear myself
being called to die in the sun's gleam
in splashing tide and bird call
sounding for fish.
All my ten fingers dig the sand.

Ocean's love is in me probing.
I am proud to be asked.
My death must count for something.
I live to find out.

■ 62.

I touch the flesh around the skeleton,
letting my hand follow its curves.
I grasp it firmly in places,
caress it where I should, probe
with my fingers where I may.
I'm delighted by the feel of flesh
and its contours, its depths,
its wetness, warmth, hair, shades
of white, brown, olive. I breathe in
its subtle exhalations. I am thankful
for the skeleton that supports my body.

■ 63.

I am alone and I feel my important thoughts
turn against me. I grow weak, fall down
and bury my face in my arms.
I shall soon pass, I cry. Release me.

And I have died and stand up, freed,
for the earth is all I know now,
its trees and grass, and I will walk
among them because they do not rise against me.

I will live to praise the earth
with my presence and give it to my children
as my gift.

■ *64.*

In this dream I do not exist. This I know since it is my dream. How have I come to that conclusion when it is I who dream it? No one else thinks I do not exist but no one has enquired because no one knows I am dreaming. Therefore, since to myself I do not exist, it is true simply because I say so. This, then, is the problem: when I cease to dream will I exist or not exist?

I would like to become nothing for the pleasure of the great leap beyond being that becoming nothing alone can achieve. I can become nothing because I am something and I am something because it can lead to nothing. Can I ask of my life more than that it bring me to its transcendence, that I should be in search of it, as the work of being itself?

My dream, then, of not existing is my being telling me where I must go and what I must welcome as the rounding out of my completeness. I say this in the best of health and in expectation of a long life.

■ *65.*

I look the sun in the eye:
Whom do you love? I ask.
The sun never replies
but I know the truth:
it loves itself,
so there: living together
in the same universe
and getting along.

■ 66. *For Stephen Mooney: 1913–71*

I saw a shadow on the wall
weeping
spreading itself
The wall darkened
and the one brightness
was the light overhead
I saw no body of the shadow
darkness was its body
needing no man no woman
and there was darkness
comforting
relieving me of their darkness

And who were the parents of darkness
I suspected the light that spread itself
absorbing
pregnant with darkness
and this is what I know
until the born dark
absorbing light
gives birth to light

67. In the Dark

I'm seated beside my phone
waiting for a call
that will tell me everything
is settled; live as you've always
wanted to, and I keep waiting.
Only nighttime brings me
to lie down, with the phone still
beside me, waiting for it
to ring in the dark.

68.

Praise the worker bees that can sting
on provocation. Praise their wanting
to be left alone in their own lives.
Praise their dedication to community
and willingness to die with the sting.

And praise the sting on my left arm.
I run as fast as I can to the drugstore
for a pain reliever, already dizzy
from the effects of the sting.
And praise the pain reliever.
It goes together with the sting.

■ 69.

Conceal yourself behind the rock
and call out his name and offer help,
your hand out thrust so that you
do not see the face or the shaking hand
and can lean back
against this rock to turn your face
up to the sun, you in your body,
and in your face and in your pleasure
and in this love. But turn to give of yourself
from behind this rock what you can give,
as the sun gives and turns away
in the evening to keep itself.

■ 70.

At night I think I will meet the one
overwhelming revelation that will set me
straight as from my youth, cost what it will,
and I make ready to grapple with it,
when peace, peace comes, though I am awed
by its night and strangeness.

It was true the earth potentially was a bomb
needing man's ingenuity to set it off
and that men worked on that prospect
in their studies and that every man
in the street was made of nerves
needing a slight jar of an elbow
to ignite him and that with the expected
death of our globe we had abandoned
our manners: we saw men's throats
cut in offices and in the streets.
Still, we had to think first
of our comfort and of our families
and the few beauties we clung to
for relief—like the bunched daisies
or the look of poplars in the rain
in a distant field. We thought they were
tall men who had come down to visit
and wore tall peaked hats against the sun.
The daisies spelled sunshine in peace,
our families of a Sunday in the congregations
of the living. Our money would suffice
until immolation and our homes stand until—
and our pleasures the same. It was worth
believing in these few things
that padded out the time
until we thought, starting,
But we are alive!

■ 72.

I live admiring the sky
and the mountains and loving
the day and the night, so glad
they are with me, my eyes open,
my nostrils breathing air,
my feet beside the lake,
the sea sound of my heart's beating
at anchor up and down
in the slow swell,
my life oceanic
reaching into the distance.

I am brother to the tree,
runner with the rabbit
who twitches his ears in the silence.
I cannot figure my own cost,
not in money, no more than I can count
the wind that wraps me around.
On my death the world will go broke,
for in me will have been poured its treasure,
and, desolated, the sun will stand
as empty as the wind.

■ 73.

I want to be buried
under the angel of a tree
among the cherubim of grass
and the lion of the wind softly
in my ear and the lamb of the rain.

I am gone.
Time has happened to me,
the minute hand on the face of the earth.
Earth is a happiness of its own
as running water
as flowing grass
as the flight of birds.

■ 74.

So many people are dead
or dying that I begin to think
it must be right;
and so many are crowding into the world
that living too must be worthwhile.

■ 75. *Midnight*

As I stood heating a pan of milk on the stove
I heard my mother's voice calling me
but I remembered sleepily that she was dead
and entered my wife's room enquiring
what she wanted. Sleepily she asked
what it was I was saying and I realized
it was not my wife either whom I had heard calling.

■ *76.*

This plant could have been a person in another age, by the process that changes coal into diamonds or persons into dust. I have this to tell it, then: I can walk the street but that is not your concern or wish in the nature of things. I also enjoy my food but again it reflects nothing of your way of thinking or living. I drink water in limited amounts neither of us can live without, so we are not all that strange to each other.

Do you know that people are killing each other in streets and trains? But I am speaking of my human condition. I could withhold water from you. I could be that kind of person, and you would die, leaving me alone with my fellow men, expecting them to do no less to me, for cruelty, like most anything that lives, flourishes on what it feeds, and cruelty, like love, enjoys its own sensations.

I think it is the caring for myself that keeps me feeding water to you every day. Plant, you can't possibly die at my hands; your death would make me desperate, knowing my own life threatened, knowing that the world would end with the demise of all plants.

■ 77. As We Walk Our Lives

I find that my life depends on a bet that I have made with a menacing character: if I pull hair out of my head three times in succession I die. The first two pulls show hair between fingers, thin, undernourished grey hair. Now I try for the third time and I'm being watched closely that I apply the same pressure against my scalp as in the first two tries. I pull. I watch as my hand comes down to the level of my eyes. I had seen a blur as I raised them hurriedly to meet my descending hand and somehow I can tell that there is a hair between my fingers, my skin sensitive to it. I look closely and there between the thumb and index finger is a hair so tiny and narrow that I do not see it except as I place it against the background of a wall. I consider myself dead, waiting for the stroke that will kill me. I am waiting, I look around me; no one is present, but who was talking to me, threatening my life? It was a voice certainly, and I begin to have a suspicion that it was me talking as usual, entertaining myself, in a manner of speaking, keeping alert to the possibilities of sudden and arbitrary unmotivated death. And now I must turn on myself and be stern. No one is threatening me, no one wants my life. I can walk the streets in safety, make distant future appointments and dine calmly at table. The world is open, as far as I wish to go. I am free and always have been.

Leave me, I tell my fear. Never return, and I order it out with a backward jab of my thumb, as though ruling out a foul play in baseball, but nothing moves. My fear does not move, and I cannot make it leave; it has no body. I cannot exorcise it; it is not evil, it is the fear of evil, and so I must live with it as company, my arm around it, its head on my shoulder.

■ 78. *The Social Life*

I find that I've been hung upside down on a hook like a caught tuna or sand shark, and people are gathered around looking me over. They come and go and children push in among adult legs to get a glimpse of me. I myself am curious about this position I'm in and can't understand how it happened. I'm not about to ask the spectators, who would think I'm stranger than they had realized, able to talk, still alive in this upside-down position. It doesn't feel especially wrong, I'm quite comfortable. In fact, it's interesting to look at people from the bottom up, so to speak. My first view is of legs and knees pumping up and down like so many machines clomping around aimlessly and bumping into one another. I'm fascinated, and sometimes I see many legs suddenly stand still in a row like a picket fence, forming a kind of barrier, as if trying to block my view of something I would want to see or that could help me set myself right side up. But then I raise my eyes to the faces above these legs and I am distressed at what I see—stares of indifference, as if a person hanging upside down in public were a common sight, as if it even could happen to them or has happened. Young couples holding hands shrug and amble off. I watch them leave, their heads turned toward one another.

I suddenly sense being discouraged and realize too that in being discouraged it could have been me who had hung myself upside down and that is what makes the spectators so indifferent. I notice several talking about me in amused tones. Well, in that case I decide to turn right side up and with an acrobatic upward curve of my torso I leap over myself and onto my feet. The crowd, astonished, begins to cheer, and some young men stroll over to ask how I had made that leap. Several girls begin to walk toward me shyly. I'm quite happy and I walk off with these young people to have a beer and to satisfy their curiosity.

■ *79.*

To look for meaning is as foolish as to find it.
What does one make of a sea shell
of such and such color and shape,
an ear or a trumpet, rose and grey?
It has been spat upon the shore
out of the sea's mouth. Is this what we mean
by our thinking? This, in wonder? So
that thought itself must pause,
holding the shell lightly,
letting it go lightly.

IV

■ *80. A Prayer in Part*

Now that we have ordered well may we turn back upon
suffering; after the fixed moments and precision, to seek
comfort in release. Peace being with us, may we flourish
in our design and discover, peaceful, that we are not hu-
man until we die; now that we have ordered all the rules
may we seek out what rules us; when we have fixed all
matter in a pattern, as who have emptied all problems
into one and made science simple, may we break down;
now that there is nothing not said or recorded and made
use of may we give back the whole thing; since we are
through thinking and all that is needed is to act, may we
sit back; now that what remains is but to live, all means
being available, may we drop them and go, go some-
where that is not calling us, that is not in us, for which
we have no earthly use at all.

■ *81.*

I must make my own sun
regularly to avoid being
lost within and frozen
to death—the poem
as I make it
out of the wood
of the forest where I wander
rubbing the pieces together
picked up
as I stumble upon them.

■ 82.

For Robert Lowell

I sit here thinking I should write,
in dread of stepping outside
the room to find nothing exists.
Here I can make something exist.
There I find myself non-existent
in doubt in empty space. Poem in hand
I can walk out of the room in safety.
I tack it upon a wall.
The emptiness gathers around it
and begins to read.

. . .

Where is the image that will free me
of the necessity of living
by taking over the hardships?

I am asking for two lives
and I have only been able to express
the longing of this one
which is called writing the poem.

. . .

My writing teaches me
how to die tomorrow
when the weather improves,
by dying with the sun,
a law unto itself
as I am: there is this
happiness.

■ 83. I'm a Depressed Poem

You are reading me now and thanks. I know I feel a bit better and if you will stay with me a little longer, perhaps take me home with you and introduce me to your friends, I could be delighted and change my tone. I lie in a desk drawer, hardly ever getting out to see the light and be held. It makes me feel so futile for having given birth to myself in anticipation. I miss a social life. I know I made myself for that. It was the start of me.

I'm grateful that you let me talk as much as this. You probably understand, from experience; gone through something like it yourself which may be why you hold me this long. I've made you thoughtful and sad and now there are two of us. I think it's fun.

■ *84.*

I came upon the poem the way the hunter discovers the animal in the bush, with shock. I leveled my sights and was about to shoot when it spoke, "I'm here to be discovered. Place a leash around my neck and we'll travel together to your house." I lowered my weapon, amazed. The animal stepped out from its hiding and stood in front of me, waiting for me to recover. We then walked back to my house, where I sprawled in my chair, unbelieving, the animal lying at my feet and looking up at me, not with adoration or servility but as an observer of another world than its own.

I thought, if I should tell others about it they would think me touched. So I decided that when they came to visit me or I them I would have this animal at my side. It might ask for food or leave to do its toilet, and all those gathered in the room would stare at it in horror, then at me, then back at the creature in disbelief, then back at me, finally to burst out, Was that speech they had heard from this animal at my feet? I'd have to nod solemnly, very much amused. Yes, speech, and the rest of the evening would go by in an uproar of excitement, delight, fear, delight, fear.

■ *85.*

*A prominent poet receives
a national award for the
perfect form of his poems.*

Hello, drug addict, can you become a poem of perfect form?
Hello, Mafia, can you become a poem of perfect form?
Hello, schizoid person, can you become a poem of perfect form?
Hello, raped girl, can you become a poem of perfect form?
Hello, dead, napalmed man, can you become a poem of perfect
    form?
Hello, incinerated Jew, can you become a poem of perfect form?
If you can't, then you don't deserve to live. You're dead, don't
    exist;
we want clean earth; get out, get going, get lost.
We have built a house for ourselves called the Perfect Form
and we're trying to live in it, and if you can't take
your napalmed body and your drug-addicted brain
and make them into a poem of perfect form then you don't
    belong
here. Go somewhere else. Go to Vietnam, where all
the imperfect bodies are and stay there and don't come back
to this country where only the poem of perfect form is wanted.
That's all we live in; you're a foreigner and we don't want you.
You're a kook and we hate you. You're a shit
and we wipe you off the face of the earth.
If you can't make yourself a poem of perfect form
then you have no right to be in this country.
You're here without a passport. You've lost your citizenship
rights. You're an alien, you're a spy.
You're somebody we hate.

Hello, poem of perfect form, we're home again to you
and we're going to snuggle up to you.
You give us so much comfort and pleasure.
We can run our hands over your darling self
and feel every bit of you; it's so sensuous and delicious;

it's so distracting from those bastards outside
who want to disturb us with their imperfect poems.
Fuck me, poem of perfect form.
Let me fuck you. We'll fuck each other.
We have each other, right, so let's do all the nasty
things we dream about and we'll have fun and nobody else
will know about it but you and me and me and me and me and
   you.
Wow. I don't want to hear another word
except your groans and sighs.

▪ *86.*

Finally, I'm sitting here at my desk because I'm afraid to venture into the street to be accosted by a person asking for help that would mean my whole life. I have only myself to spare and I need it to help me. Those who cry out for help have somehow lost themselves, given away or simply been robbed. I have to stay at my desk to keep myself as I am, though it's little enough, but it gives me my presence and place to be.

It is a selfish act, if I can read your thoughts, and I am ashamed, but I am fearful too to act on my impulse to love, the love for others to which I bow my head but refuse to honor because I'm afraid to love beyond myself. I know this, as my heart pounds when I get up to step outside. This is my love, I confess, and I shall remain here to write of it as my acknowledgment, to get it out for others to see and understand. They may knock on my door and ask to be let in. I may let them see me crouched over my typewriter, fearful, showing them my back, but glad that they have come to see me writing of my love, my one way to express it without losing myself in their arms.

■ 87. Epilogue

The trees are tall gods
commanding a view
of my study. I bow
my head over my typewriter
and start the ceremony
of a prayer.

Whisper to the Earth

To the Memory of
James Wright

I

■ *My Own House*

As I view the leaf, my theme is not the shades of meaning that the mind conveys of it but my desire to make the leaf speak to tell me, Chlorophyll, chlorophyll, breathlessly. I would rejoice with it and, in turn, would reply, Blood, and the leaf would nod. Having spoken to each other, we would find our topics inexhaustible and imagine, as I grow old and the leaf begins to fade and turn brown, the thought of being buried in the ground would become so familiar to me, so thoroughly known through conversation with the leaf, that my walk among the trees after completing this poem would be like entering my own house.

■ *Autumn Leaves*

This time I can't grieve
over their deaths in yellow and wine red.
The tree bark is light gray
and a blue jay has just swooped in
to land on a branch, shaking leaves
loose. They do a dance on the air
as they fall.

■ *Behind His Eyes*

A man has been tied to a tree and thinks he is beginning to feel something of the tree enter his body. It is hard for him to discern what it could be, but he would like to grow tiny branches from his head, and leaf buds.

He loves standing still. He thinks he can feel the tree pressing up against him, as if it were trying to instill in him its nature and its seed. He is in a kind of trance about himself. Thinking, as he had sensed before, is no longer a function of thought but of action. That is because he has welcomed the possibility of tiny branches and leaves that now he believes are growing from his sides and from his head. He would laugh in pleasure but that he finds himself swaying back and forth as in a dance that could have been induced by wind.

He is very happy, very much the tree, and he has shed his alarm at having been tied to it in the middle of the woods and left to die. He can forget the reason for his captivity which he thinks of no longer as capture but as a piece of luck to have happened in the midst of this crisis in his life. He is free of crisis, and can celebrate by bringing forth more branches and leaves, and he straightens up from his now stooped posture of exhaustion to let new growth emerge more easily from his head and sides. He is alive and that is what counts, alive in a form he has always admired, and now it is his and he is glad, only to find himself growing more sharply stooped and losing memory of himself, as this last thought becomes the bark he has seen behind his eyes.

■ *The Tree*

Looking out on it from my window
I feel contiguous with it,
perhaps by our common air
in each other's presence.
Here, as proof, is this thought,
the one most intriguing,
for in one leap I stand
outside myself, seeing myself
from a tree's standpoint,
and I do look peculiar
moving about.

■ *A Cloud Creates*

A cloud creates the face of a man who, happening to look up, recognizes it as his own. The face under stress of the wind begins to disintegrate into wings, and the man sees in himself the ability to fly. He stretches forth his arms and waves them up and down as he begins to circle and dip as a birdman would in the currents of the wind, and then the face vanishes and the wings drift apart, too, in shreds and patches.

The clouds darken, as they will; thunder rolls from their colliding with each other. Lightning flashes. He knows he is at war with himself, the reason for which he cannot go into at the moment.

There is no consolation, not until the rain ceases and the sun emerges and once more clouds arrive, white, brilliantly lit, and so for him full of hope. He has not attempted to sort out his, as it seems, random feelings since sighting the face. And though there is no order to his feelings, of that he is certain, he needs none, not while the sun rises and sets and weather prevails. It is from weather that he derives, and so he has no faults. He is without fault, he is of the weather.

■ *To Oneself*

Admit the sky carries no threatening message
in cloud or color. The birds wing by,
your only disturbance and pleasure. The grass
gives you gentleness and the earth selflessness.
You are encouraged on all sides by the impersonal.
Admit: the grasshopper sways upon a blade of grass,
men rest themselves upon the flood.

■ *In No Way*

I am of the family of the universe, and with all of us together I do not fear being alone; I can reach out and touch a rock or a hand or dip my feet in water. Always there is some body close by, and when I speak I am answered by a plane's roar or the bird's whistling or the voices of others in conversation far apart from me. When I lie down to sleep, I am in the company of the dark and the stars.

Breathe to me, sheep in the meadow. Sun and moon, my father and my father's brother, kiss me on the brow with your light. My sister, earth, holds me up to be kissed. Sun and moon, I smile at you both and spread my arms in affection and lay myself down at full length for the earth to know I love it too and am never to be separated from it. In no way shall death part us.

■ *Tomorrow*

I exist without the dignity of stone
that does not bother that it exists,
and so let me place my hand upon an open flame
and cry out my pain because I exist.
What other is there, without an open hand
into which the apple falls at end of autumn
or that cups the rain of a summer sky
or opens to the sun or moon? I am
the door to tomorrow.

■ *An Ancient Fable*

A swordsman came charging out of his castle with sword unsheathed, wildly swinging at the air. He would slay air. It was the cause of his enemy's being alive. If he could not meet him to cut him down, at least he would destroy his enemy at the source. He charged into the open meadow, thrusting, parrying, shouting execrations at air for ignoring him, for giving him to breathe too. But air was not to be killed by the sword, and so he rested. If there had to be enemies, then there had to be air also, or he too would die. He had to accept his enemy as he had to accept himself, as he had to accept air and water too. He was thirsty from effort, and there on the opposite side of the brook he saw his enemy stooping to drink. He waved at him good-naturedly. "Do you know we are part of nature and that it is as natural for us both to be enemies as it is natural for air to be and for us to breathe it in?" The enemy looked up from his drinking, released his short knife from its belt, and flung it with great force toward the opposite shore, where it plunged into the chest of the swordsman, to his surprise. He sank to his knees in horror, in disbelief, in anger and in sudden understanding that he had suffered the evidence of indifference in nature, and as he died he was glad that he could die free of anger, free of shame at his death.

■ *The Apple*

The skin also wrinkles in old age,
the meat still sweet, if less plump,
and one eats it casually
out of the bowl
where it had been sitting
with other wrinkled fruit.

It's what the apple would want
if it could speak—to be enjoyed—
and one chews and enjoys
while chunk by chunk it vanishes
into the eater's mouth noisily
and is fulfilled.

■ *The Eternal Men*

The eternal men are deplaning at airports, briefcases under arm, arriving from a sales pitch or a conference on application of scientific discoveries. They are sober with the experience of thinking, debating, deciding and explaining, and are anxious to sit down at table to forget themselves in food and drink. They are tired and reluctant to state what life seems to them at this time. I am standing behind them, my face aglow, my body of light, and I am whispering of pleasure in my youthfulness: I have given up caring and thought. I am intoxicated with myself, and they are growing restless, hearing my voice as if in sleep when they are helpless. They turn on their seats to look into each other's face to study if what is happening there is what they are hearing. I continue to whisper that I have penetrated their thoughts the way the sun penetrates a curtain at the window. I will light up their days and nights. I will make them restless for the balance of their days to go out and meet the sun as they travel in their hired cars and on their working flights to conferences. I am, and they are yet to become, yet to discover it in their sleep made brilliant by the sun of the memory of their youth.

■ *In the Garden*

And now I wish to pray and perform
a ritual of my devotion to the sun.
I will bow and sing beneath my breath,
then perform the dance of farewell
and my confidence in the sun's return.

All is dance: the sun glides along the horizon;
now the leaves sway;
now the earth spins.

■ *Of That Fire*

Inside I am on fire. Imagine, though, coming up to City Hall and asking if there is a Department of Burning Need, ready for emergency, I the emergency. I can see myself being locked up gently in a madhouse and declared as finished in this world of material evidence. Are my clothes on fire? Is my hair burning? Are my cheeks aflame? Do my feet scream with pain? My voice is calm and my clothes intact, my hair and face moist with sweat, and the oils of my body—normal. "Where is the fire?" the cops will ask sarcastically, giving me a ticket for speeding my brain beyond the legal limit and remanding me to court. I will plead guilty and admit to it publicly, for I'll have no evidence but my spoken word, and all the while I'll know the cop, the judge, and the jury are burning within too, without a shred of evidence either. They'll laugh and shake their heads and signify with a twirl of their fingers at their heads a crazed man before them, which will show how sane they are, not knowing they are dying in the fire that was lit in them, born of that fire.

■ *Here It Is*

This is how I felt as a child:
I was high on self-delight
at the touch of the mild sun and breeze.
Here it is Spring again
and I have lost my sixty-fifth year
in the blinding sun.

■ *I Dream*

I dream I am lying in the mud on my back and staring up into the sky. Which do I prefer, since I have the power to fly into the blue slate of air? It is summer. I decide quickly that by lying face up I have a view of the sky I could not get by flying in it, while I'd be missing the mud.

■ *Each Stone*

Each stone its shape
each shape its weight
each weight its value
in my garden as I dig them up
for Spring planting,
and I say, lifting one at a time,
There is a joy here
in being able to handle
so many meaningful
differences.

■ *If Trees*

If trees that are lesser than I, so it is said by others, respond to Spring with an offering of leaves each season, can I do less than offer at least one poem in praise of breathing at regular intervals?

■ *For Yaedi*

Looking out the window at the trees
and counting the leaves,
listening to a voice within
that tells me nothing is perfect
so why bother to try, I am thief
of my own time. When I die
I want it to be said that I wasted
hours in feeling absolutely useless
and enjoyed it, sensing my life
more strongly than when I worked at it.
Now I know myself from a stone
or a sledgehammer.

■ *I Identify*

I identify with the wooden shed in my neighbor's back-yard and with cords of wood neatly piled. I am identified with the necessary, whether I myself am necessary. Why does a man go on breathing when he is in despair? How would it help to know, consciously, clearly, rationally, but what is rational about the necessary? If to live and have pride in oneself is rational, then the necessary is rational. I say to my neighbor. I hope that you will have a warm fire from those cut logs and that your wooden shed will keep your tools clean and safe from dirt and frost, and I begin to feel myself bodily alive again, proud to have a body like any shed or cord of cut logs.

■ *Growing Up*

II

These were among my first thoughts on earth: I have been placed here as some kind of reward, given the gift of being what I was, and I loved my bike, praising it for moving at the command of my pedaling, and steering in the right direction at my touch. The sidewalk lay flat and still, expecting the bike. It, too, cooperated with the powers that are, and no one stood in the bike's path to topple me over. The wind upon my face was like the hand of approval. Where then was my change hiding, my hidden change?

I never thought the bike betrayed me, nor the sidewalk, nor the wind, but now I see them simply as means, and I am the betrayer. I cannot call the bike an emissary. It is a tool, the sidewalk a path, the wind a current of air. We are no longer communicating that I'm aware of, but what does it matter, I tell myself, so long as I am free to use all these for my delight. But I am alone in my pleasures. I am not the child of anyone, for, as I watch myself growing up, the bike shrinks in size and the sidewalk fills with cracks and bumps; the wind on my face in cold weather chills me, and when I eat I know it is because of appetite.

I have become something no longer at one with bike, sidewalk and wind. I can feel cold, hunger, appetite, the self and all that this means—because the bike is never hungry nor does the sidewalk ever have to go to bed, and sometimes the wind stops blowing and for me does not exist, which earlier, would have frightened me about myself, while the wind never is frightened. It never speaks about itself, as I am beginning to speak about myself, and so I know there is something about me very different. Sometimes I am panicky about it, but more often I am glad because I have still another thing to turn to in pleasure, and that is this self which is always with me, but I am alone because a tree has begun to look lonely to me standing by itself, whereas once I had thought it beautiful, saying what I felt about myself too—that I was, that we both were. Now the tree looks lonely, but I know that that also is my thinking, and the thinking is my pleasure and my burden too. I am all alone, and so I turn to another like myself and find him happy to turn to me.

And now we have begun to differ about the games we should be playing or the places to visit on our bikes or the time to go home for dinner. I become lonely again, my self needing to be defended as my only absolute friend and sharer, but my friend and I exchange smiles often and talk together with gentleness and teasing and wait for the voices of our parents to call us separately to dinner.

■ *Ah, Room*

Ah, room, you wait for me day and night,
faithfully silent, expecting no reward
and, if I do place a picture on your wall,
you become so beautiful to look at
that it is I who am rewarded by your beauty.

You are so selfless, it is hard
for me to leave and visit other
and stranger rooms where I am not
as comfortable as I am with you
though they are fancier and even more
imposing, with furniture and lamps.
It is because of this that I am
not at ease as I sit there thinking
of you with bare floors and mostly

bare walls, undraped windows,
like huge, solemn eyes to look out
on the busy world. In the midst of luxury
and laughter in ornate rooms, I long
to return to you. With you I can indulge
myself in sadness and in loss and feel
your self neutral in my presence
and ever willing to accept my thoughts
aloud, tears, my frantic phone calls
for a voice to speak to me
in my loneliness with you. You do not
protest, you are not shocked, you are not
unhappy with me, as perhaps you would be
in rooms so much more appointed and decorous,
where smiles and graceful gestures
and good, witty talk are in order.
You do not harbor a grudge for your poverty
of chairs and tables, carpets and silken drapes.
You wait only for me, and I arrive
almost anytime, even in the early hours
of the morning, yet you receive me
silently, openly.

If that is love, then I am grateful,
and, if my feelings towards you
partake of that sense, then I am
a happy man. So together may we
last through other nights and days.
I will play you music on the radio
or turn on the TV for your pleasure.
Together we will view and hear
the world as lovers do, from a distance
of exalted ease in each other.

■ *The Window*

The window was made in an effort to be free of brick walls, and it succeeded, but I do not see a face behind it. Still, it is a window that offers hope of another face, and from time to time, when I remember, I show myself at the window in case someone is standing behind the curtain who needs the courage to show himself or herself that I can, by standing in the light, supply.

■ *Solitude*

I am sitting here alone because
it is important to overcome,
as catastrophe, sitting alone.
I believe it is just as good
as being seated in a crowd,
and I would prove it
by being seated with my sense
of togetherness with others
so that I may write of being
alone in a communal sense.

■ *But I Can Act*

I am looking around for an exit from my loneliness that is like the vast, open, flat land of Kansas, gray sky, flecks of blue showing here and there. How do I find an exit from an untracked land? But a voice within, my voice, of course, keeps urging me to start walking. Which way? In any direction, the voice answers, and so I pick myself up from the ground where I had been sitting cross-legged, thinking, and begin to walk. I pass snake and badger holes. These animals live alone. I keep walking, there's no end to the horizon, nothing there to greet me that would take me out of myself, but to walk has become an activity. I am sad, but I can act.

■ One Leaf

One leaf left on a branch
and not a sound of sadness
or despair. One leaf left
on a branch and no unhappiness.
One leaf all by itself
in the air and it does not speak
of loneliness or death.
One leaf and it spends itself
in swaying mildly in the breeze.

■ *Company*

I am a cripple, my two arms hanging down over my head
from the elbows. I have to walk that way, as if they were
partially raised in despair with things as they are. But to
have to walk through the streets with my arms raised
above my head brings me the stares of strangers passing
by. What could they think except that I am one of the
many mad that walk freely through the streets, or a pro-
phetic figure, which sets them to tremble inwardly, just
after having received their latest bribe or their most re-
cent prostitute. I suppose I could be some sort of message
that allows me to walk through the streets with a show
of confidence. But, when I am alone in my room, what
then? I look in the mirror and frighten myself with my
forearms dangling over my head, and I become severely
depressed. Is this my fate from now on, I ask, to have my
arms above my head in a gesture that could mean total
despair? I am alone, and so I rush out again to find people
with whom to mingle in the street to share my misfor-
tune. And should you be one of those who does get
to see me walking with my two arms dangling above
my head from the elbows down, I live to receive your
stares of sympathy, awe, terror or hate. I do not pass judg-
ment on you and, if you should find it in yourself to see
me as but a human being in trouble, think of me as com-
pany too.

■ *I Am*

I assume a Buddha-like expression in the mirror.
All that is needed now is to remove the doubt
lingering in my eyes, staring back at me
with amusement. It could be the Buddha,
all comprehending, entertained
to see me wish for that
which already should have been.

And so I am not he, nor can ever attain
to his role, but that he could shine
out of my eyes in the mirror tells me
he exists because I wish for that
which, as Buddha, I should have become.

I am, and so Buddha and I are not one,
but this is for my human self
to know he exists and that I exist
in his eyes and am understood.

■ *I'm Sure*

I'm sure trees are depressed also; they are so silent except when the wind blows, but notice how abundantly they grow their leaves and how tall they manage to become, thick around the waist like wrestlers. They wrestle with the wind. I could learn from them. Their leaves rattle and hiss among themselves as if leaves are grown to express depression. But see how thickly they grow upon the branch and what shade they give to persons passing or seated beneath. It's an odd function for a depressed tree. I was about to try a razor on my wrist.

■ *Dream*

I am lying face up on a raft
floating upon a lake. The waves
are small, rocking me gently.
I am myself, in love with ease,
my arms and legs loose, my breathing
so low I study my being alive.
And at last, invigorated by my ease,
I turn, cup my head in hand
supported by an elbow against the raft,
and search the woods and waters
for a friend or stranger
with whom to share my self.

You wait in a rocking raft
or lie close against the ground
like its lover.

■ *A Modern Fable*

Once upon a time a man stole a wolf from among its pack and said to the wolf, "Stop, you're snapping at my fingers," and the wolf replied, "I'm hungry. What have you got to eat?" And the man replied, "Chopped liver and sour cream." The wolf said, "I'll take sour cream. I remember having it once before at Aunt Millie's. May I bare my teeth in pleasure?" And the man replied, "Of course, if you'll come along quietly," and the wolf asked, "What do you think I am? Just because I like sour cream you expect me to change character?" The man thought about this. After all, what was he doing, stealing a wolf from its kind, as if he were innocent of wrongdoing? And he let the wolf go but later was sorry; he missed talking to the wolf and went in search of it, but the pack kept running away each time he came close. He kept chasing and the pack kept running away. It was a kind of relationship.

A Requiem

My father, listening to music, that's me,
my legs outstretched upon the bed
as I lean back in my chair. I think of him
in his chair, legs crossed carelessly
and with his musing smile recalling his first wish,
to become a baritone, his smile seeking
after his youth or watching it in the distant past,
untouchable. I am alone, and the opera playing
heightens my loneliness, without son, without father,
without past or present, and my future a problem.

Eh, father, as I listen to your favorite opera
you would have enjoyed my listening and approved
emphatically, while I'd withhold myself,
tentative towards opera, as other matters burned in me,
such as the need to be free,
and so we would argue but soon fall silent
and go our separate ways.

I am alone in my apartment, alone as you were
without me in your last days at about my age.
I am listening to Rossini and thinking of you
affectionately, longing for your presence once more,
of course to wrestle with your character,
the game once again of independence,
but now, now in good humor
because we already know the outcome,
for I am sixty-six, going on sixty-seven,
and you are forever seventy-two.
We are both old men and soon enough
I'll join you. So why quarrel again,
as if two old men could possibly settle
between them what was impossible
to settle in their early days?

■ *Cockroaches*

I have become friendly with baby cockroaches that dare to come out in the daylight to see what am I cooking or peeling. They're like little children curious about their elders and would like to know. I watch them scurry about on their invisible legs, they are so gentle and enquiring and frightened. When I raise my hand or lower a spoon they race off to a crack in the stove fixtures. Occasionally I crush one with my thumb on an impulse and go back to my cooking or peeling potatoes.

As for their parents, long as the first joint of my thumb, when I turn on the light at night I watch them in anger. I begin to spray with a poison. That their deaths will diminish the birth rate of their children does not bother me. It's the horror of their aggressive search for food that I react to viciously.

I leave the kitchen with its noxious poisonous smell and forget about their struggling death to listen to my radio, to read my book, to do my schoolwork, to think of how empty is my apartment with just myself in it, sick of being alone, always alone and not knowing how to change it to a life of friends.

While my father walked through mud
in shoes borrowed from his sister,
all Kiev attended *Prince Igor* and cheered,
and while he worked in a cellar bindery
and slept on workbenches rats leapt over
at night, Dostoevsky's *White Nights*
and *Anna Karenina* were being read avidly
amid joy, tears and protests. My father
was the silent one, walking through the streets
where the hot arguments went on about poverty
and guilt. He walked, his work bundle under arm,
from cellar to monastery, to bind holy books
and volumes of the Russian classics,
and when they had had enough of classics
and needed blood, he fled,
for his blood was real to them; only he
had worked and starved. All others were
but characters in a novel or a play—
bless Chekhov, Gogol and others for their genius,
but my father was the one who had not been
immortalized and made untouchable.
Only he was real in Russia's torment.
Only he stood for life. All else was books,
and that was the torment.

■ *Thus Truly*

The sounds of labor in the street, hammers at work to open pavement, ignore me. Everything is itself and so must return to itself after the event toward which it travels, as does the hammer that strikes at the pavement repeatedly but takes on nothing of its grayness or concrete strength. One resists while the other insists, and there is no meeting of qualities that each could appreciate and want to share.

I am striking at myself to open and plant a tree or make room for my friend who then I could say was a close, loving companion, going with me wherever I must go. This is what it means to be alone.

What keeps me intact after each strike is to know that my face has taken on the shape of each blow, and when I meet with others we measure our suffering at a glance. In deepest secret we are each other's subject of pain, thus truly as one.

■ *Preparing*

I'll have to see my father dead
and I just know
that I do certain things
to live. Beyond that
are wordless men
doing the work they have to:
murder is one
and loving is another.

■ *A Life of Wonder*

I am alone with life, but we do not talk to each other, as if life were waiting for me to come to an end of my performance of itself. It stands by silently and aloof, leaving me to fend for myself.

I would guess that this is all life has to offer, and yet it must offer itself to become, and so I am the life it is.

I am wondering, but life is not. I am asking questions of it, but life is not, as if it has enough to do handing itself from person to person to keep itself alive.

Is it possible life is unhappy with itself? It does not speak except as I speak, and does not act except as I act. It has no independence other than what I do for myself. It is a puppet of its own making and allows me to be the one to manipulate the strings.

I am life, then, in fact; and I am the one who should speak to me. There is no one else, even if I were to speak to friends. We would be speaking to mirrors, and so I can deny or reject myself or make do and make merry with myself. I can do each on alternate days, not to neglect any one choice, since as life I must be as life, impersonal in my choices. I am happy indeed with this discovery, a discovery it is. I am a life of wonder at myself.

▪ *Kaddish*

Mother of my birth, for how long were we together
in your love and my adoration of your self?
For the shadow of a moment, as I breathed your pain
and you breathed my suffering. As we knew
of shadows in lit rooms that would swallow the light.

Your face beneath the oxygen tent was alive
but your eyes closed, your breathing hoarse.
Your sleep was with death. I was alone
with you as when I was young
but now only alone, not with you,
to become alone forever, as I was learning
watching you become alone.

Earth now is your mother, as you were mine, my earth,
my sustenance and my strength,
and now without you I turn to your mother
and seek from her that I may meet you again
in rock and stone. Whisper to the stone,
I love you. Whisper to the rock, I found you.
Whisper to the earth, Mother, I have found her,
and I am safe and always have been.

■ *The Ship*

I saw an ocean liner in the desert, its crew leaning over the railing, as though the ship were plowing through the waves of sand. I was reluctant to ask how a ship came to rest in the desert. The world itself was strange enough, and I did not want to ask questions that would make matters worse. I hailed the crew from my position on the sand and asked where the ship was headed and was answered promptly, Into the desert. I asked to come on board and at once a rope ladder was handed down. I climbed eagerly; we would go through with this absurdity together since, after all, it was our experience, and we could help each other to live it through.

■ *The Bread Itself*

Mother, in my unwanted suffering,
I turn to you who knew suffering
like an odor of food and breathed it in
with that familiarity. I can learn
from you to become my self, eating my sorrow
with my bread and gazing frankly at the world
as a man, as you, a woman, taught me
by your silence and acceptance of sorrow,
the bread itself.

■ Father and Son

A black man is hugging me around the throat from behind with his forearm as he demands in a rapid undertone my money. I think of his embrace as nearly an affectionate one, as if from a son who has come up from behind to demand his stipend for the week in a playful imitation of a mugger. I turn carefully as I would to a son for whom I have the greatest affection and say gently, "The money is in my breast pocket," and I make a motion toward it with my hand. He strikes my hand, as if carrying on the game of mugger, in case, as in the game, I was reaching for a gun. I say again gently to my black son, "The wallet is in my breast pocket." He does not smile. He lets me reach into my jacket to bring forth the wallet, which I do, and he snatches it from me. The game between us has become serious. I am in danger, but I react with calm.

Is this my son, this tall, husky young man who is extracting the bills from the fold and now returning the wallet? I am cautious. I did not train him to be a killer or threatener, but he is serious about the money, and he pockets it all. I have an empty wallet that I return automatically to my breast pocket. He and I look at each other. I think I have a smile on my face, and I think he sees it and is mildly astonished, and maybe understands it or is curious to see a smile. We look at each other for another moment. There is curiosity between us. This is not my son but another man's, and he is acting towards me as a stranger. We are strangers, but we are to each other in the relationship of father and son by age. He opens the door to the elevator and orders me in. Will he kill me in the elevator? I look into his face; he must realize what I am thinking. He holds open the door, waiting for me to enter, not threatening me, simply waiting, and I enter. The door closes behind me. I look through the porthole to see him looking back at me. Is he taking a last look at the man who could be his father whom he has subjugated to his will? I think I am still smiling. I think he is smiling back as the elevator begins to climb.

III
■ *Hairs*

I am studying the hairs from my head that I was able to pull out gently this morning, as I do each morning instead of combing. Gray hairs, white hairs. I'm not convinced that I am old and that I should resign myself to finishing my days in quiet and calm. I continue to tug at the hairs in my balding head to find those that are firmly fixed in my scalp.

■ *Above Everything*

I wished for death often
but now that I am at its door
I have changed my mind about the world.
It should go on; it is beautiful,
even as a dream, filled with water and seed,
plants and animals, others like myself,
ships and buildings and messages
filling the air—a beauty,
if ever I have seen one.
In the next world, should I remember
this one, I will praise it
above everything.

■ *Walls*

In a clay pit he sees himself trying to climb out, the clay clinging to his feet keeping him down. He's puzzled, not very anxious, doesn't seem to be suffering from hunger or worry about dying in the pit. Just wondering whether he'll be able to get out. He tries again, fails; his feet can't detach themselves from that gray mass avalanching beneath the step that he takes to mount one side of the pit, and now finally the clay has buried his feet, and yet he wonders how it is that the clay supports him in his upright position.

That's it, to stand still, as he is forced to, and spend his time looking about at the sloping walls and on the natural designs of their uneven surfaces. And for how long will he stay here, he asks himself vaguely, as he concentrates on the walls. He has no answer, his question muted by his study of the walls.

■ The Law Has Reasons

because roads lead to towns
and do not generally end up in marshes
or deserts and because there are men
in session. Each morning they comb their hair
before the glass that shows the fine vapor
of their existence; they sit in chambers
for its exact word, neither sullen
nor filled with despair: dust too
must be as dust underfoot or on table
each morning wiped with a cloth clean.

▪ *This Body*

This body on which I counted for an eternal life, this
body with which I strolled out into the street to glory in
the breeze of a summer sky, this body that will make me
to lie down among the dead, that will close my eyes and
close down its heart—how a body can do this to itself,
having loved its own pleasures, enjoyed its own excite-
ments, having sought after new ones every day. Yet it is
ending itself too and I am caught in the middle, asking,
Why can it not be consistent with its own love of its
pleasures and go on, go on? I stare at it in the mirror and
I look down on it naked and see nothing to have warned
me in the past of its decision to be finished at a certain
time, the legs sturdy, the thighs muscular, the stomach
flat and hard.

It has stood in the fields at night to look up at the stars
and count itself among them proudly as a body too glow-
ing within, radiating its pleasure in being alive, to which
others were attracted to make a pact of friendship and
identity—this body intends to end itself in the ground
beneath a pile of dirt. It will not listen to my pleas, to its
own pleas, as I hear them repeated within me and echo-
ing in my brain. It expects to die. It does not know
whether it wants to die but I do know it intends to die,
as if it were obediently following instructions like a sol-
dier on the firing line who sees the prisoner, his best
friend, tied to the stake but who is waiting for the order
to fire. He will fire, he will grieve in silence, he will re-
press his grief, he will forget his friend.

In Memoriam

(Al Lichtman)

He stood with two-wheeler between us,
cuffs pinned by clips
to keep from tearing on the sprocket;
I looked away. In the house we had sat
seeking each other's pattern
with feeble light: words about the weather.
We had lit ourselves, fixed in perpetuity—
he rounded, easy to start, hard to stop;
I, rough all over, bogged down in my rudeness.
He had talked as if it were a plan for paradise.
I sat stolidly, like an egg flattened
on its bottom.

       He arose, sensing the loneliness
made with one's private eyes; and I, conceding that,
arose to say good-by. With a two-wheeler between us,
he let me feel where I had failed him,
his brown eyes vacant.

      . . .

Death has given him what he had sought,
a perfect amiability with life,
all other friendships failing.

■ *Pretend You Are Asleep*

If you look closely at the exhalations of my inner heat
distorting the air around me, you will see I am burning;
my eyes shine, my skin glows, I move legs, arms, head
and body restlessly as fire. Have I burned others? I can
assume I have. Have I been burned in return? That's
when I burn brighter.

My flesh one day will have shriveled towards my bones,
my bones turned brittle, my mind shrunk to silence, my
spirit low as ashes. Ending in my own fire, I will have
resolved myself into an image: "I live for you, I burn for
you, I burn my self. Keep alive, and when nothing else
helps, close your eyes, pretend you are asleep."

■ Elegy for Youth

I trembled when I heard the news.
Who else must go, I finally asked myself,
to prove the world is temporary.

Good-by, young man. In your grave
I want you comforted in your silence
that this old age is but the absence
of youth.

Very much alike is our condition,
except that I must feel it
all the short days that are left to me.

We traversed the distance between us
on the bridge of our smiles. You saw me
as old and kind, and you I saw as understanding
my wish to be kind, not to talk
of growth and decay, my life simplified
by its coming death, but you went before me,
and now that you have led the way,
I may follow without fear,
your gift to me.

■ *Respected Graves*

I am seated on a chair resting upon a wooden floor supported by a concrete foundation poured and sealed into the earth that whirls in space without visible support. I am quite worried. This whirling sphere does not know its own future nor its past, and is traveling at a reckless speed into the dark. I hold my breath, expecting to crash at any moment with a star or comet, but I can't hold my breath for long, and I begin to breathe in trepidation.

And here I thought I could take pride in my ancestral beginnings, the history of my tribe, their complications, their rise and fall, as if they had been the real beginning. My lordly Indian killers, god keepers, makers of cloth and slave runners, all who endured their life's darkness are traveling with me in the dark in their respected graves.

■ *Street Scene*

Now the steam hammer is still
on Easter Sunday, and the steel girders
are lined up alongside each other
like witnesses of their own lives.
Tomorrow they will begin their descent
into the ground like gods
who need to be buried in ceremony
so that all can witness and say amen.

▪ *I Saw a Leaf*

I saw a leaf flying in the opposite direction from the ground, but there was no wind. Now how could that be, I asked myself. It was a dead leaf, shriveled and brittle looking, one of the many hundreds that were dropping to the ground off the trees beside my house. Puzzled for an explanation, thinking perhaps an updraft had caught the leaf and sailed it into the sky, I watched it grow smaller and smaller to the eye, and soon I could not make it out at all. I shrugged and entered my house and closed the door behind me. I could imagine the house beginning to take off too, and I sat down as if to pin it to the ground, when, as I seated myself, there was a tapping on the door. I was expecting company. I approached and opened the door. A single leaf lay on the doorstep at my feet.

Between Shade and Sun

I'm alive to prove the existence of death in me too,
I'm alive to make death visible to myself and to others,
and I think that to be alive with these thoughts
is to be experiencing death at the same time.

I go from one thought to the other as in a walk
from the dark side to the sunlit and back to dark
when the sun grows too hot for my uncovered head—
uncovered in honor of the sun, when as it starts to burn
my scalp I know it is time to move across the street
and into shade. I walk until I tire of the cool,
once more longing for the sun, as I gaze
upon its brilliant pleasure in itself.

I commute between two worlds
and expect to succumb in time to one or the other,
for if I linger in the sun too long
the shade will come upon me from within
and if I walk in shade I will grow cool as death,
but having walked in both shade and sun
I will have lived forever
in seeing nothing change but variations
in the change from shade to sun.

■ Between the Living and the Dead

If there is anything to life
besides living it, we would know,
wouldn't we, by something
going on inside, like a loud hum
of urgency or an illumination
of our insides day and night?
But since we just sit or eat,
then go to the toilet
or make love and get dressed,
are you disappointed?
Do you wish to rebel?
Will you write out a protest?
I wish I knew what I could say.
I too am sad, I write it out
to leave it all behind
for others to give it thought
that will make a bond
between the living and the dead.

■ *A Catechism*

Do I feel a moral outrage about immoral acts? No.
Am I a friend of the people? No.
Do I believe in justice and mercy? No.
Do I have a love for others? No.

Do I have a love for myself? No.
Do I live out of love for the world? No.
Am I a happy man? No.
Am I desirous of the happiness of others? No.
Do I look forward to a future of peace and plenty for the world?
    No.
Do I contemplate the destruction of the world? Yes.
Do I hope for it? No.

Am I looking forward to my own death? Yes.
Am I hoping for it? No.
Am I enjoying my life? Yes and No.
Is there anything I want to say before I die? No.
Do I feel satisfied with what I have done in this life? No.
Do I expect to see an improvement? No.
Is there a possibility in my mind that such an improvement can
    be made? No.
Doesn't that upset me and make me sad or depressed or want to
    get myself to do something about it? No.
How do I manage to live in this kind of pessimism?
I contemplate it.

■ *Improvisation II*

H   I always speak with the voice of God.

How's that?

H   Because he wants me to.

Do you mean he lends you his voice as he remains silent?

H   Exactly. Isn't he nice?

I should say. I wonder what he could do for me, if I asked.

H   What have you got on your mind?

I'd like his authority and power.

H   Well, why not ask him?

O.K., I will.

H   So ask.

Oh, do I ask you?

H   Yes, of course. I am the voice of God.

I see. Well, you're also human, so you're not going to give me the authority and power.

H   By no means.

Then why did you want me to ask?

H   So's I could say no and show you my authority and power.

I believe you.

H Do you want me to demonstrate to you, anyhow?

Sure, go ahead.

H O.K. Disappear!

Who?

H You!

Me?

H Yeh.

Disappear? What do you mean, disappear?

H I mean disappear, vanish. Get lost.

By whose authority?

H By mine.

Make me disappear.

H But you don't understand. When I speak it's to be listened to and obeyed.

I see, the voice of God.

H Exactly.

O.K., I'll tell you what I'm going to make disappear—my foot up your behind, I'm going to kick your ass so hard!

H Don't you dare!

Why not?

Because I'll tell on you.

Oh, you will. Who'll you tell, voice of God?

I'll tell myself.

I see. And then what?

I'll get mad.

And then what?

I'll disappear.

You'll disappear?

Yes, I won't be around any longer.

You'll leave me.

Yes.

You'll take the voice of God with you.

And leave you alone, all by yourself, to worry and take care of yourself.

Is that so?

Yes, and you'll miss me and cry for me and have no one to turn to for help and advice and prayer.

I'll pray anyway.

But nobody will listen. There'll be nobody to hear you.

Oh yes, I'll hear myself and so will my neighbors, if I'm in a group.

And you'll be praying to nothing and nobody because I won't be there. I'm going.

Wait.

Why?

You're funny. Stick around.

And then what?

O.K., we'll pray to you and listen to your advice and laugh.

How's that?

O.K., laugh, but don't expect to get results.

O.K. We never did anyway. You're one of us.

Oh yeh? I'm the voice of God.

And so am I.

Why?

Because I feel like it. I feel like you.

Oh.

Yeah, now you pray to me and like it.

Pray to you? I'm the voice of God.

So am I.

So we're even.

O.K., we're even. We're walking, talking voices of God and we can communicate with one another. How's that?

Great.

We'll tell each other fabulous things.

We'll give each other great dreams and emotions and futures and we'll be happy in a dream.

Hey, man, we're making it together.

What do you know!

We're pleased.

We're content.

We're special.

We're peculiar.

Why?

Because I said so.

That ain't enough.

Well, you say it too and it'll be unanimous.

A We're peculiar. We're ourselves. We're anybody we want to be. We're the voice of God. We have his authority and power. Because we say so.

Aren't you tired of this game?

H Oh, is it a game? I didn't know.

Know any other?

■ *Crystal Chandeliers*

I wait for the mailman.

Why do you wait for the mailman?

He gives me something to anticipate, the opening of letters, finding bills and reminders of sales and notes from friends to say hello and what are you doing and why don't you write or come for a visit or can he come to visit me or he may have something to say about a mutual friend divorced or remarried or a success at love or publishing. Something, that is what I am waiting for.

Well, may I wait with you, then?

Is there going to be mail for you too, in my batch?

No.

Then why wait?

It will be nice watching you open your letters. It's something to anticipate, as you say, and I would like to enjoy it along with you, or if that's too personal and intrusive I could stand at a distance and just watch your face as you read each letter.

Oh, then your watching me will add a new wrinkle, as I watch myself, a double perspective.

Right, and then I knowing you are watching me watching you will add yet a third perspective.

Exactly, and knowing that both of us will be watching each other will add yet a another dimension.

Imaginatively

Intensely

With pleasure.

And perhaps in fulfillment?

In us.

And around us?

In awe

In worship?

Godhead.

Paradise.

Hell.

Purgatory?

In letters?

They'll be coming from humans like ourselves, with their own needs and joys, pleasures, identities, dread, happiness, terror and wonder.

At sending letters?

Aren't we altogether in this?

Giving each other love, hate, bills, friendship and gossip.

Forming a circle of ourselves.

A mystery?

An awesome awareness. We live in a circle.

Of millions of bodies and brains and always with the same image flashed back to us, the same thoughts and emotions.

Is this happiness?

Is this with dread and expectation, fear and joy, love and hate?

Is this the life in which we stand in awe?

Yearning for more of it.

Yearning for ourselves, more of ourselves, always more.

Centered upon ourselves and emerging from ourselves to converge upon ourselves.

Renewed.

Refreshed.

Or hurt and sad.

Or killed outright.

By the hand of another whom we know to be our self turning against us.

Divided from ourselves

Bent on suicide.

What should we say to all this appalling commentary upon ourselves?

We must think.

The letters have arrived. Here is the mailman.

Good morning, Mr. Mailman. We are very pleased to see you.

Thank you, but I get paid for doing this.

And we are grateful there is money with which to pay you.

Otherwise I would not be here.

Really.

I'd be out looking for another job.

And what about our letters?

Good-by, Mr. Mailman.

Did you see him shrug at my question?

And he did not even say good-by. Now I am sad.

And now perhaps we can make ourselves happier with the opening of these letters.

The better part of us.

We are turning around and around like a crystal chande-
lier, showing to ourselves all our lovely and unlovely
parts.

It will be nice watching you open your letters.

Crystal chandeliers.

■ A Discussion

I'm looking for the idea of order.

Where are you looking for it?

Under the table.

How about the closet? Or under the bed? Or in the kitchen sink? Or in your pants pocket? Or in your wallet? Perhaps in your head?

I can't imagine finding it there.

Well, have you looked in the jails?

No, but I have looked in the bars.

How about the grocery stores? How about the banks? Or a garage?

Or a skating rink?

We'll find it, keep looking. You're not doing any harm.

And that's good?

What would you call it?

A kind of order.

An idea in search of its order? I know that in my mind I crave it.

And in my mind I miss it.

That's saying the same thing.

Of course, and I just remembered that there once was a woman with a very hairy face. I remember her from my childhood when I went with my father on a visit. I was struck dumb and all the way home later I could not say a word to my father as I kept thinking of this hairy face.

And that to you was a sign of disorder?

Yes, and I remember on a stroll with my father up the block we lived on passing a jewelry store with a man seated at the window repairing watches. I turned to my father and I said, I am going to become a watchmaker when I grow up. He smiled and said, Yes? And I nodded vigorously.

And that was a sign of order?

Yes.

Do you recall what happened to that hairy lady?

No. She was married to the house painter to whom we had gone to make arrangements to paint our house. He seemed not the least upset by his wife's appearance. And that felt like . . .

Order?

Yes.

So there was both order and disorder in that house?

I don't know whether that actually was the situation and I can't believe it can exist, given the same condition for both in the same place.

Then must we say that we don't know whether there was order or disorder or both?

Right.

And we don't have any solid answer to go on?

We're in the dark.

And all is as if back in a kind of first chaos.

Right.

And we have to live with it.

Right.

And make our peace with it in some kind of order.

A very tentative and problematical kind.

As for your ambition to become a watchmaker, did you become such a person?

It left my mind as soon as I became interested in something else.

And so you lost at least one idea of order through your own thinking and found yourself thinking of another kind of order.

I have forgotten what that one was.

V
■ *Want Ads*

Two lovers with little to say to one another begin to quote from the headlines of the day's newspaper, and their excitement mounts from the front page through Sports and Finance, but when they come to Want Ads the sounds they emit to each other over the phone are simply indescribable. They have found their love again in its primal state and, as they are about to swoon with recovered ecstasy, they turn a page and come upon the Obituary Column. They have much to grieve over, and grieve they do for each other's coming end and absence from this life, which will leave each lonely without the other.

Is there consolation for this loss of happiness and pleasure and, of course, joy in each other? They turn the pages of their newspaper languidly, once again in their misery. It is an absent-minded act as they turn, and they come upon ads for furniture, clothes, vacations, for the lastest dance records and night clubs, for the latest styles, and they begin to glow. They can spend money, shop for a house, for a car to drive south in the winter; and furniture, a crib, attic space, a garden for vegetables and flowers—all as advertised in the newspaper. Two who could not be happier, their love again spontaneous with pleasure in each other.

■ *On Freedom*

In a dream I'm no longer in love. I breathe deeply this sense of freedom, and I vow never again to seal myself in, but I am reminded it is myself I love also and that too is a kind of sealed condition. I am committed to taking care of my body and its home accommodations, its clothes and neat appearance that I admire in the mirror, yet I would like to know what it would be like freed of brushing my teeth, washing my neck and face and between my toes. I'd like to know, as I neglect to move my bowels, and stay away from food that could sustain my health, and do not change my underwear, and let odors rise from my crotch and armpit. I stick out my tongue at the image in the mirror showing me my ragged beard and sunken eyes and hollow cheeks, free of my self-love at last, and I sink onto the bathroom floor, feeling life begin to seep out of me, I who haven't eaten since last month. I'm dying and I'm free.

■ On Censorship

A man, a famous man, is being talked about in another country and, because he is being talked about, an official from the Department of Culture has arrived at his house to strike him for each thought expressed by the stranger on this famous man. He asks, Why strike me when it's not I who is doing the talking? We strike you, the reply goes, because you are the surrogate for that man. When he stops talking about you, we will stop talking to you with our hands. The famous man decides to call up this stranger whose name he does not know and ask him or her to stop talking about him, and so he places the call with the operator, who says she knows exactly who the stranger is and that she is ready to call the person but first must strike herself over the head, as required by the rules of the Department of Culture. This she does and then proceeds to put through the call. The person answers the phone, listens, and gives one huge scream, which is heard by the famous man, who turns to the cultural attaché of his government and says, That person knows my work. I am delighted.

■ *The Interview*

Dear fellow gull, a question or two for you to answer, if you care to. You're up there banking and floating in the wind. Is that for the pleasure of it or do you have something else in mind, such as spotting clams from that height? Secondly, as you walk along the shore, is that just for pleasure of walking or are you feeling with your feet for something to eat? The last question, what kind of soap do you use? We are advertising Cleano. Have you used it yet? Oh, you have and you say it tastes good? That's great. May we quote you? Thank you. There will be residuals from this. We'll be able to pay you for your endorsement of our product each time it flashes on the screen. We can send it to you in cash or in clams. You prefer clams? That'll be easy enough. We'll hire your fellow gulls to dig them out for you and provide them by the bushel. Oh, you don't want that? You've changed your mind? You want my bald head on which to drop your clams from a height. I can send you as many bald heads as you wish but you must excuse me if I withhold mine. You see, I'm program director and without me we can't get you on the screen with your commercial. You want me to resign and come live with you? I might try it someday but you must excuse me now, I must take your answers to the studio. You'd like to drop my head from a height and open it like a clam? (At this point, one hundred gulls are observed taking a good grip on the program director with their beaks and lifting him to the sky and releasing him in the air! He's still dropping. They catch him as he's about to land, fly him up into the air again, and release him; this time they mean to watch him land!)

■ *I Love to Fly*

In a dream I am making phone calls to dozens of airlines to find out the exact flight time to cities all over the world and enjoying the sounds of Amsterdam, Bangkok, San Francisco, Peking. I gloat at the thought of being in flight, seated luxuriously in my 747 and drinking vodka martinis, wines, liqueurs, soda pop, coffee, tea and malteds. I am many different kinds of persons, you see, because I cannot contain so much joy in myself alone. Finally, where do I want to go, these many different persons that I am? Mexico, Japan, England? Name the country, the city, the open field, the cliff, the mountain, the riverside, the ocean or the cave. I am confused; my many different persons make so many conflicting requests. I should go to Malaysia, but I hear my other selves sing Hong Kong, Ceylon, Indonesia, France, Africa. What do I do? It's not a matter of money. Sitting here and envisioning my trip doesn't cost a cent, but I want to go to one place at a time, explore it thoroughly, and move on from there. "Malaysia, please. Round trip to Malaysia." I am confounding all my other voices by deciding on Malaysia, and they are unhappy, which means I ultimately will be unhappy. Could I carry on a life like this, as, for example, loving one woman but hearing my voices suggest a dozen others all at once? This is madness. It certainly isn't middle class. What do I mean by dreaming all this? I should awaken and get rid of such temptations. I should awaken. All my other voices are in disagreement with me, and I love to fly.

■ *The Reply*

I am the chair he sits on at the desk to type his poems and letters and comments on himself and others, a strange man. He can actually fart while typing the most soulful lines. I'm used to it and anyway—what can I do to stop him or protest? I creak, I bend, I roll from beneath him and he promptly jerks me back toward the desk, a stern taskmaster.

What I'd like to do is write my own poem about him, but here I sit in front of the desk and typewriter in his absence and simply comtemplate the idea. My two arms rest at my side and refuse to move upward to the keys. What could I write about except about being a chair, previously a part of a tree trunk? Which was the better fate? I can hardly judge. My life is already fixed in its condition—to serve others—but I should take that as an omen of good. He does find me of value. Yet think of what will happen to me when he becomes too old to type! So we have something in common, don't we?

I wish he would recognize that and stop farting on me so that at least I could respect myself as he respects himself. Does he? We're equals in the end, aren't we? He should know that, being so smart as to know exactly what I'm thinking now, while he's typing my thoughts. I don't even have my private mind hidden from others, which shows you how much a slave I am. Does he have pity on me at all?

Oh, I do.

■ Now I Hear

Now I hear two unsynchronized steel hammers pounding on steel, making contrapuntal sounds between them, as if to teach me the first simple lesson about order, that there are many kinds, and that two could cause discordancy between them as harsh as war; and now one hammer has stopped and it seems as if the other is pounding away even more rapidly to gain on the other if and when it starts again. I sit at my desk waiting for the answer, but now the silence is complete, the second hammer fallen silent, and I am left at my typewriter to make the necessary sounds that we associate with life.

■ *With Horace*

With Horace I take my stand beside the rocks
and clear falls. I will not be confused
by sound or the stone's hardness. Voices
emerge from me and hardness takes from me
its quality, for Horace lived upon a mountainside
and made shapes that were not pliant.
He dug for rock, as I am, of the born elements
compressed. Did he crush his wine grapes
underfoot? Did he mix with the rain
and the rivers? Who gave him grapes to grow?
Hard money. And am I sick, then, being happy?
He entered a stone house and struck off
his fire upon stone.

Leaving the Door Open

To My Parents
Yetta
and
Max

Arjuna Said: *Seeing my own kindred here, O Krishna,*
desiring battle, ranged against each other,
My limbs sink under me, my mouth dries up,
trembling besets my body, and my flesh creeps.

My bow Gandiva slips from my hand, my skin
burns with fever; I cannot stand, my heart
is confused;

I see contrary omens, O thou of the flowing
hair, nor can I look for the better part,
if I slay my kindred in battle.

Bhagavad Gita, Book I

■ *I.*

He got his friends to agree to shoot him standing against a stone wall, somewhere in the country on a deserted farm. It was to resemble an execution, the plan cleared with the police, at whose headquarters he had signed attesting to his desire to be shot and, in clearing his friends, declaring his death a suicide that they were to help him to—at the peak of his strength.

Never to return to life in any form but that of earth itself, since earth was not fearful or joyous. And then he was followed, on inspiration, by his friends, one by one, each fired on by a diminishing squad until the last left was shot, as a courtesy by the police. Afterward, the police shook their heads, puzzled, grieved and somehow angry at those bodies lying sprawled with outstretched arms and legs against the ground, as if pleading with the earth to let them in.

■ *2.*

Here comes one of my kind. It's night, and I am caught in an open, deserted parking lot as I approach my car—a man, and I should not be afraid of what he may want to do to me, a man like me, with feelings of fear, hatred and love, and with a desire to live, like mine. I should greet him aloud as I would a long-lost brother or friend, recognizing him in the dark after all these years. I should feel good about it, welcoming his identity. I should not think he is about to rob or perhaps kill me, I should smile at him as he approaches.

■ 3.

For Neruda

Soldiers surround the house of the poet and crouch, their guns poised in his direction, but do not move, held by their awe and fear in his presence. He comes to the window bitterly to look out upon his own people in uniform, with guns pointed at him. Bitterly he stands there and they, crouching, are more deeply silent in the anguish of their taut faces and eyes. He is their poet who speaks for them in his poems, that they have read and heard over and over, swaying to the rhythm of his lines.

He flings open the window where he is standing and shouts, Shoot, shoot me! They recoil in a body, except for one who with speed and reflex of long training at command raises his rifle and pulls the trigger. His comrades bury their faces in their hands.

■ 4.

Two men wrestle on the ground.
Whoever is pinned beneath
can glimpse the stars
and the steep night,
friends lying dead beside him.
Whoever lives will walk alone
past silent fields and houses.

As they pant and lunge for the throat,
rolling one on top of the other
across the ground, the fight grows
more formal, in contempt. They
have stared into the other's eyes
and seen one who can respond
to hatred or to love.

■ *5.*

I crawled over the dead bodies and moaning mouths of the dying to get to where my family was alive, hidden in its cave. I had been in search of food and firewood when I discovered I was in the midst of killers laughing and competing. I hid under a pile of dead heaped over me that I had dragged by the legs and arms to cover myself from head to feet, and I lay down, not breathing as the killers strolled by, jabbing idly with their knives at the dead. When the field grew silent, I cautiously made my way home on my belly, in case they in the distance looking back at their work could detect an upright, moving form.

Now I'm back with my wife and child, and we hug each other in silence from time to time, grateful to be alive, yet sick to our stomachs, unable to eat what I have foraged. Should we too die, we ask ourselves silently, looking into each other's faces? It seems so commonplace, after all those who fell like so many apples shaken from their boughs, but we drag ourselves over to the food and force ourselves to eat. Especially I urge my child, insist, command, threaten with punishment, and she submits, crying, and stuffs the berries into her mouth, chews sullenly and swallows.

■ 6.

As he passes his hand over his face in front of the mirror in a gesture of weariness from the day's work, he sees he has wiped off the right cheek, with its bristle of hairs and its curves, to leave a solid as smooth as a billiard ball. He stares, wonders at how weary he must be to have to see this. He passes his hand over his left cheek, with the same result. He is alarmed at himself and questions his balance. To prove himself wrong in his suspicions, he runs his hand swiftly across his eyes, and they are wiped away, leaving him blind.

He screams, but he is alone. He would stare at his hand, but he cannot see; and he rushes madly out of the bathroom and into the living room, banging himself against the furniture. He is terrified of himself; his hand is his enemy, his destruction, and he holds it at a distance from himself rigidly, frozen in his fear, but in a burst of anguish he rubs his two hands together wildly, as if to wipe away the crime, and they wipe each other out, leaving him with two plugs of flesh.

He wishes to destroy himself, mad with grief. With the loss of his two hands, what worse can follow? And he passes the right plug of flesh across his head of hair in exhaustion and in horror he can feel the hair disappear beneath his touch. Insane now, he forces these flesh plugs to pass over each part of his torso and with each touch that part is wiped away. He laughs, out of his mind. He runs his plug down his legs and across his feet, and he falls to the floor with a crash, legs and feet giving way, no longer there. He begins to flop on the floor like a fish cast upon shore. The door to his apartment opens and his wife enters, observes him tossing himself about, tangled up in his clothes, and is silent.

■ *7.*

The sweetness in a man, the very one about to set out to kill a stranger in the forest for poaching his preserves of wild animals, vegetation and fruits: he plays upon his clay pipe melodies about himself: his love for children, wife, tribe and land. It sets others to listen, nod and glance at one another knowingly and to focus on him the more closely to hear how he reaches them in their feelings about themselves and their affections. He gathers spear and sword in his hands and steps softly into the woods to kill. He grinds his teeth in expectation of killing with a fury that will brook no resistance of the creature he is after to make it die in its blood.

Later, he will take up his clay pipe to play in the knowledge that he has killed one that delighted too in the fruit and vegetables of the forest and that loved having been born into its offerings. He will play and perhaps call it a prayer to the mystery of having to live and die in a surrounding of plenty that never in itself will die, as if to dream one could take from it the power in food to live forever but for some baffling reason is never to happen. As he plays, suddenly, because he cannot solve the mystery of his own eventual disappearance, perhaps by the spear of his enemy, if not age—suddenly, in frustration with the question, he will begin to dance, to dance out the disappointment in thinking, in questioning, in searching in himself for an answer. He will dance unto exhaustion, and all who have been listening to him play since the beginning, startled to see him rise to his feet to dance, will join him, his bafflement theirs, as it conveyed itself to them in his playing from the beginning.

■ *8.*

This newspaper states that Idi Amin killed over one hundred thousand Ugandans last year. How did we manage to do that, Idi? I am an ordinary man, I enjoy my food; I love to make love. How did I manage to kill that many? I remember, calm now, at peace with myself after a fine meal, my violent temper, my tantrums, my sudden turn to cold calculation to kill those tribes—men who oppose my rule. Not openly but by practicing rites forbidden them. They raise gods and magical powers above my rule. I cannot be threatened. I am growing furious again.

How many have we killed, Idi? I have here a report that these same rites continue to be practiced in the bush. Hunt those people down, I command; slaughter every one of them. Pull out their fingernails; crush their balls in your hands, and women—crush their breasts between your fingers until they burst. I am Idi Amin. And bring me my wife; I want to make love again to forget those fools who would oppose me. I have to shake my head. I am a man like all men.

. . .

Idi, I dance with the dancers, sing their songs, drink their wine and mingle among them with my broadest smile. I enjoy the wine and comradeliness of bodies with which I feel at one, of my kind—men, and any one, as I look him in the eye, I barely restrain myself from shooting, so much do I fear him too, who would kill me to take my place.

Idi, the dancing increases in violence and meaning. I watch myself dance in their bodies, and I know I am frightened of myself in their bodies, as they are frightened of me in their tumultuous rhythms, but I am, and I am who must live myself.

Dancers dismissed. Guards, surround me; I am returning to the palace to brood on death.

Here in the palace, Idi, I ask myself why do I think this way, and I answer myself reassuringly: power is beauty and beauty is what I am after, that which I feel in my marrow when I exert power. Then I transcend myself, I become the power, and I kill to make my beauty blaze.

I forgive myself, there is no one to take my place, for I am; therefore, I must be Idi Amin.

■ *9.*

He is searching inside his body for the cause of his depression. It's as if he were searching with his hand from organ to organ in his chest. He can feel depression near his heart but, as he moves ever so cautiously in and around that area to grasp that ache and extract it, nothing comes to hand.

He conceives of it as something living within him illegitimately, and, since he cannot remove it bodily and has addressed his plea to it more than once to remove itself from him, he believes that now he has the right to do it violence, to drown it, and he begins to drink.

He becomes a fog to himself, the heavy mist that rises from his drink in conflict with the inner warmth, and he no longer can detect specific depression. It is now a general fog and that, of course, is as nature can be in unstable conditions. He thinks himself a fact of nature, and he travels unsteadily, as fogs do, from street to street, from house to house and, like fog, finds himself locked out from these houses or hurried past.

It is night. Fog, through which all things must enter and pass, can be dangerous. Vehicles are traveling at high speed, and fog is pierced by lights, by people and by trucks. He is knocked down and crushed. As mountains are shaken and torn down and earth opens, his death too is a phenomenon in nature. Affirmed in his being, he rolls over on his face to die.

II

■ *10.*

My uncle smoked his cigarettes down to the last half inch and served cherry jelly with crackers and tea on Sunday to his guests. He was methodical about costs. And I used to climb the tree for the cherries. The crackers and jelly were hard to come by in quantity for my hunger. Just a handful of biscuits on a plate and one small jar that made the guests feel greedy after two helpings. Uncle would look on approvingly and smile and praise his jelly, homemade off the cherry tree. No sugar on the table for the tea, not with jelly.

As for his wife, hands folded in her lap, she sat apart without comment, for her husband knew how to make money, a stubborn man for bread and cheap cuts and so there was cash for mortgages in the neighborhood: old-law tenements and clapboard two-family structures with worn wooden steps. Their landlords came to his hardware store for supplies to be charged double for postponing the interest on their mortgages.

On Sunday it was all family, in summer especially. Everyone sat at the round, green, cracked table between the garden and the back entrance to the store, a concrete patio with straight-backed, round-bottomed cane chairs. My father and Uncle Philip and Aunt Bessie, my mother and Aunt Pesha and Uncle Hymie and cousins Archie, David, Frieda, Fay, Dora, Bertha and Alex—together running in and out of the garden, climbing up the tree, pushing the lawn mower across the grass and eating the crackers and jelly. I was hungry for food but, my father heatedly defending the democratic cause in the last war, my uncle's wisecracks interested me, he who owned the garden and the store.

■ *II.*

Here in bed behind a brick wall
I can make order and meaning,
but how do I begin? How do I
emerge without panic
to the sounds and mass
of people in the street?

Are they human who stare
as I pass by, as if sizing me up
for a mugging or a filthy proposition,
and am I human to have to be
frightened and on guard?

It's people I'm afraid of, afraid
of my own kind, knowing their angers
and schemes and violent needs, knowing
through knowledge of myself
that I have learned to resist,
but when I can't I have seen
the havoc I have made.

It's this, knowing their desperate motives,
as I have known mine, I'm afraid of
in them. I hide upon a bed
behind a brick wall and listen
to engines roaring up and down
the street and to voices shouting
to one another and find no meaning
or order in them, as there is none
in me when I am free of self-restraint.

The bed is my victory over fear.
The bed returns me to my self
as I was young and dreaming
of the beauty of the trees
and faces of people.

■ *12.*

I find you at twenty-six
seeking refuge
in drugs and hospital routine,
the same son I raised in anger
and self-pity who is without hope
of a life free of me and I know
we both are in trouble.

■ *13.*

I no longer want to feel with you
your tragedy—if but for a moment
to experience death. That cannot
bring home a salary, a toy
for my child, a poem to tell
of my life with or without you.
I will be known for the steadiness
with which I carry grief,
so that one could use me
as a pillar for a house.
And since this tragedy is for us both
you will see me in the distance
walking firmly, so that you
will want to follow,
leaving death behind.

■ *14.*

Stranger in my life,
I will take care of you
even after my death—to whom
I give the feeling of a father
to his grieving son, for whom
the father will do anything
to make him live.

Stranger,
the cause of my bitterness
at your condition, and my strange pride,
you my son since no one else
comes to claim you and since I
am sworn to myself to give you all
a father can: love, pity and faith.

■ *15.*

You are totally helpless in sleep
and yet I cannot enter your thoughts
or your innermost desires
as they're evoked in dreams.
We remain apart and I am a man
lonely with himself and in need
of another.

I fold my hands in my lap
and wait for resignation
to announce itself in me
and with it an acceptance
of another self that writes
this observation in silence
and in pity.

■ *16.*

I named you my son, then withdrew
and you have been searching for me
ever since, with anguish and confusion.
Here I am, you think, reaching out
and catching yourself, about to fall.

■ *17.*

Whatever contribution I was to make to living
has been made, yet living has gained nothing
from it but a sharpened sense of its futility
for me. The robin hops from branch to branch
as if one branch makes a difference over the other
and hopping in itself is important to the cause.

Standing idly at the door to the meadow,
not knowing of anyone in need of me,
made unwanted to myself, I glimpse
my neighbor standing in his doorway
too and staring out.

■ 18.

The dog's bark that sounds as though it were choking
on its own grief, I hear it nearly every night
before bed and take it into sleep
to name a part, I know,
I would prefer to lose—that part
I won't recall except reluctantly,
as if I were to face myself in something
hopeless of correction, yet must be felt
again because I am the guilty one
for wanting to escape that grief—
unhappy, coughlike bark at night,
and night is dark enough to keep it hidden,
but night is when it happens
and where it lives.

■ *19.*

There is a fault in the universe
that I should have the fault of self-doubt.
The constant exploding outwards
into space, as if to occupy it all
to leave no room for doubt.

If there's no end to space,
then there is no end
to explosiveness, and to racing outward.
With space finite, the universe
will turn in on itself, crushing
each particle of self in search
of assurance, constancy, stability.

■ *20.*

What kind of life is it for a bird that lands upon a branch alone, followed directly on its heels by another, with cries of delight or anger between them, a sort of scuffle I hear, as in an attempt at mating—and away flies the bird that followed, leaving the other by itself, alone again perhaps to perch in its aloneness. It too suddenly flies off and pierces the air in the silence to a new branch or whatever.

Where then is the flock with which to join up and be consoled, or what is it that birds do to fortify each other in their desolation? Is it instead this aloneness, and for that bird, too, that followed in the silence of a hot afternoon of sky as clear, as firm-looking as blue marble?

■ *21.*

Lying quietly on the bed
I've become an object of the room
the way my book in hand exists
from moment to moment, its contents fixed.

How lovely it is to exist as an object.
How sweet and tranquil are the filing cabinets
and ceiling. I have found in myself
their separation from thought: never confused
in themselves or seen by others as anything
but what they are
to the touch and to the eye.

■ *22.*

The language among the clashing winds
and falling trees is action, unexplained
to me or to themselves and unmediated
by feeling for or against—neither
open to discussion with others
nor with themselves. That leaves me
tongue-tied and in a hurry
to secure my safety within
my house, and the trees bend
ominously toward it
beneath the violence of the wind.

No, it's no use longing
for lyric joy, sorrow or fear. It's
no use longing for words of love
or pleading. It's simply to act
as do the trees or the wind:
to become an agent of that force
that could save my life,
and so I become impersonal to myself,
a mind of the wind.

■ *23.*

The bird was flying toward me
from a distance and as it drew near
to where I stood watching
from behind the deck window
it veered off into the woods
as if I were a stranger
among the grass and flowers.

One bird giving me an insight
into its reasoning
could make me feel at home.

III

■ *24.*

How the zebra died in the mouth
of the lioness after a brief struggle
of the legs, and then the herd went back
to feeding on the grass nearby
while the lioness and her cubs knelt
at the body as in worship
and ate their fill.

They were soon quiet and resting
on their full bellies and looking
steadily at the herd feeding itself
with heads down to the grass,
not minding the lioness or her cubs.

It was a reassuring sight,
that there was death
and that it had its place
among the living, and a time,
and that time had passed
for now.

■ *25.*

The dog barks and is for the moment a dog heard.
The child cries and is for the moment a child heard.
Also, there is the lover swearing his oath.
Silence falls on each, and the thousands
of dogs, children and lovers pass by silently.
They could be shadows.

There is no turning
each to the other: "We are all lovers,
love me in return; we are all children,
love me as a child," or "We are all dogs,
let us bark together in that pleasure."
They are stilled to have found themselves
among their own kind in troops of thousands,
and when one dog barks or a lover speaks
his oath or a child cries, it is passed over
as an anomaly, a pretense
at being a dog or lover or child.

■ *26.*

You are unhappy with the way things
have turned out for you and for others
close whose lives touch yours
and turn it from its path in the sun.
You are now with your back to it
and looking down at your shadow
stretching before you
at your feet, long, dark and sad,
you make of it a matter
for philosophy.

■ 27.

The steam hammer pounds with a regularity on steel I should envy. Neither the hammer nor the steel seems to be suffering from this terrible meeting between them, proving something vaguely pointed, that some things must be done, regardless of cost, and finally the cost too is absorbed in the doing that has become a ritual between two fated opponents.

■ *28.*

He has come to the conclusion,
walking between the empty lot
and the stone heap, his arms filled,
that this is the life. Stones fall
from his loaded arms and bruise
his feet. He trips. He could
pick flowers, he could heap his arms,
but with stones there is
always the danger,
the need to be alert.

■ *29.*

How good it is to feel the joy at last
of oneself. It is like the full moon
shining down upon the dark trees. It is
like lit trains sliding by in the dark.
It is the light of houses in the distance
punctuating the night.

■ 30.

He is hobbling along on a wooden leg, with cup out-stretched, seeking compassion and love for partnership in his grief at his crippled condition, each penny dropped into the cup a token that he can treasure and add to the sum needed.

Very little is offered, a penny at long intervals by someone who seems more concerned with his own state of mind, as if reminded of an unspoken, unacknowledged guilt, some lack in himself uncovered. The man with the wooden leg keeps limping along. At least, he thinks, he is among people and is not being removed and isolated by a cop, and he can guess that this is the real and secret offering, the tacit knowledge that he belongs; that if love, compassion and partnership are what he seeks, he is receiving them from many silent eyes that look in passing, letting his image sink into their thoughts like a penny.

■ *31.*

Wherever he looks, standing still in the city,
are people born of coupling, walking in gray suits
and ties, in long dresses and coiffed hair,
speaking elegantly of themselves and of each other,
forgetting for the moment their origin,
perhaps wishing not to know or to remember.
They dress as if having been born in a clothing store.

They were born of men and women naked
and gyrating from the hips
and with movements up and down
and with climactic yells,
as if losing their lives
in the pleasure and so glad,
so wildly glad.

From this rises the child
from between the wet crotch, blood and mucous.
He stands upright and pronounces himself
humankind and steps from bed and clothes himself
in a gray suit and from the next room of birth
steps a woman in a long dress. They meet
in the corridor and arm in arm walk its length
in search of one room, empty of inhabitants
but prepared for them.

■ *32.*

He was caressing the back and shoulders
of the woman seated beside him, his head
turned toward me in conversation, when
this woman started from his caress
and observed quite casually she was not
his wife, who without his knowledge
had changed her seat and was laughing
at him from across the room.

■ *33.*

At table they talked of family and kids,
of friends and happenings and argued versions
of the world and of events they read about
or had experienced together. They found it hard
to reach agreement on the issues and let them
fall away in silence as they ate. They were
together not to quarrel or to discuss
but to seek to make a wholeness
with each other and wholeness was the silent issue
they would not debate, since nothing else
could substitute for two together
and then they talked of love and sex
and there agreed, not saying so,
how they together were expressed in this
and so they quipped and teased
and silently agreed to go to bed,
with dinner done, and there perform
the rites of two, freed of loneliness
to make themselves the host to one another.

They came at him with crooked teeth;
he had over his eyes, it seemed, the film
of the newborn, who sees objects as emblems
of light moving upon the film's surface.
His senses pleased by light and such symbols
that announced it, he followed it devotedly,
sensing form that sought his attention
persistently above all others, in hovering
over him, in offering him objects from its hand:
gifts, some filling his mouth with sweetness,
others eliciting a joy for their guessed-at
usefulness to him. In the forms swelling
to meet him, in the eyes that were soft
to rest his gaze upon, he sensed a portent
of pleasure greater than any he had yet attained.
It was disturbing for what he sensed
of the pleasure such softness emphasized.
He was not loath to accept, his eyes still filmed.
There was light and light glowed
and with but light to go by he too shone.

He first felt their teeth when they came at him
quite close, breathing upon his cheek.
He had no fear of that. He preferred it,
and then their teeth as they pressed upon him
ripped open this film. Light was not lost by it.
Light remained and grew explicit at last
in the sight of strands of hair and foggy teeth
parted by gaps. He had no revulsion.
He was excited by particulars. Light
held everything as before but not everything
was an emblem; the shapes were not of the light
but distinct organs revealed. He examined
these revelations for detail to satisfy

his new wonder, and there was this new thought
pieced together of these details: they
were organs working together to form one object.
He had no revulsion towards this object.
He was instead drawn to it for the continuity
he now needed to establish for always,
as he had established light at the beginning,
these differences: these strands of hair,
these parted, creased lips, those foggy teeth.

He learned to love them as he loved light
for they were what made light transcendent
by being form and volume. He learned to consider
them as darkness, delightful; they gave comfort
by touch. His film gone, he believed now
in comfort, and light being everywhere
as the disturber: it belonged to nothing
yet was everywhere. Now that the film was gone
light was not all happiness, and the details
of an object were more restful to contemplate,
and he has called them in approval, darkness.

■ *35.*

Outside his window a woman washes her window
so that sitting alone she may look through
and be seen clearly. If he should turn his back
still she would be there
as he would be to her
and she would accept his back
as that part of himself
that by its nature has nothing
to say to her but presence.

Neither one of them is ever alone
in a sense that could be frightening,
such as facing the stars
in an empty meadow, with no one
aware of one's presence, with no one
curious about one's absence
so that one does not exist, except
in one's own mind that is frightened
of itself in a silent meadow
facing the stars that to themselves
are adequate.

■ *36.*

Here he is, sitting quietly, enjoying
his own presence, for it turns out
from many quarrels and separations
in himself has come an understanding
that he is the one
with whom to sit at peace silently
in friendship, or to converse.

■ 37.

He is digging his own grave a little while before he expects to die. After all, it will be his last residence and he has always built his own before. He does not want to be carried in a coffin. He will walk when he senses himself dying, and will climb down into the grave and stretch out, with people looking on: relatives, friends, creditors and those indebted to him. He will have forgiven them their debts, again to show himself free, since to die does not mean to become a tree root, or simply food for the mice. It is a stage one comes to, as at the end of a friendship or love affair when either lover or friend moves out, leaves the country or goes elsewhere. There will be that same change within, or in the grave, if he can no longer detect this change; it will be change nevertheless, and change is what he always knew above ground.

Did he always recognize himself, as when before the mirror he found himself growing aged and could not connect that with his once youthful, full face, but he was aware, and now he can expect the change that will come without his being conscious of it, but he knows of this change; he is informed. Do we not make chairs and tables of living trees? And he hauls up a large chunk of dirt with his shovel.

■ 38.

I am a vase holding a bunch of flowers
in my depth, with water in it. I enjoy
the branches leaning against my sides.
They make me feel myself.

See how tall and straight I stand
with blossoms above me. Could anything
be more beautiful than I who am nothing
but an enclosure upon emptiness?

IV

■ *39.*

Do you know I love you?

What can I do about it?

Doesn't it make you feel good to know?

No, I don't love you.

Then why not enjoy the thought that I'm in love with you?

If that makes you feel better . . . I've got troubles of my own. I too want to love someone. I don't mean to hurt you, but you're not my type.

I see. What is your type?

Oh, I don't know. He has to come on in a funny way, maybe look at me or say something suddenly that gets to me. I have to suddenly realize that this is the man I want.

Is he tall or short, dark-haired or blond?

I wish I knew. I'm just waiting for him to come along.

And then what will happen?

I'll be happy.

I'll be glad for you.

Thanks.

And when I find someone else instead of you—it hurts me to say it, it's hard to believe, I don't want to believe it has to be anyone else but you—you'll congratulate me, too.

I sure will. I'll be very happy to see you happy.

We'll both be happy, won't we?

Right.

And we'll be able to talk to each other so friendlylike and intimately about each other's happiness.

Yeh.

Whom do you think I ought to fall in love with again instead of you?

Oh, I don't know. It could be someone you like, I guess.

It would have to be, or I couldn't fall in love. Well, can you picture with whom I could fall in love?

Probably someone like me again who has a different feeling about you from what I have.

I wish I knew where to find her. Imagine finding someone just like you. I could dream all the time it was you, who had decided I was the guy, after all, who had come along suddenly to make you feel that something different.

Yeh, that would be funny.

Do you know anyone who looks like you?

No.

I don't either. How about you acting that role for me? Let me hear how it would sound.

What do you mean?

Just pretend that you suddenly found in me the man you want and act it out.

How do I do that?

Oh, I don't know, just act. Haven't you ever pretended anything?

Sure.

Well, that's it.

You mean put my arms around you and coo into your ear and all that?

Yeh. I want to see what it would be like to have someone like you in love with me.

That's crazy.

Yeh, but it would be fun for me, at least. Here, take this arm and place it around my shoulder and this arm around my waist. And now say something in my ear.

Like what?

Oh, anything, something soft and nice.

You playing some kind of game? I'm not in love with you, remember.

I didn't forget. Sure I'm playing a game. I want someone like you in love with me, and you're playing the role. Now you have to kiss me.

What if I don't?

Then I'll be terribly unhappy again and won't have you to help me imagine that I finally found my girl.

But what about me, looking for my man to love me?

O.K., I'll pretend to be that man. Then kiss me, too.

You know what? This isn't too bad, you and me like this.

Let's keep it up.

O.K., let's keep it up, and we'll make each other happy, pretending that I have the man and you the woman you love forever. At least I know you love me, so I have that to bank on.

And you're satisfied to stay with me for the moment.

Maybe longer. Who knows?

And I have that to bank on.

You know what? I think we're both happy.

Let's go to my house.

I'd better pack my things.

That was a real problem, and look how easily we solved it.

By putting our heads together.

■ *40.*

My hot-water bottle, my latest love,
when it grows cold I won't have any sad feelings
because I'll know I need only pull out the stopper
in its head and pour out the cold
and pour in the hot. My ideal love.
It couldn't possibly leave me, either,
and when I grow tired of it I can put it aside
and forget it and the bottle would never mourn
or make me feel guilty.

But what when it springs a hole in its side
and begins to leak? Then I'll think
it does not want to stay with me any longer;
that it wants to be left alone
to grow old and rot and be thrown
on the garbage heap, and I'll be sad for it
and have to think of getting a new hot-water bottle.
I'll be the one who will mourn
and the bottle will be left with no feelings
towards me at all. You can't win.

▪ *41.*

I'm lying in bed looking up at the ceiling,
asking what the limits to pleasure are,
as I feel rising within a need
to grasp a hand in my hand
for its firmness and form,
our faces turned up to see clouds
and sunlight merging, then sailing apart:
beauty and then rupture,
as it is within our grip upon each other—
to make of it that kind of love
between two selves that must break
apart to be what they are.

Everyone touch everybody's lips. It's ritual, it's important. Now form a circle, everyone, and look at each other. What do you see? Another person, naturally, but what else? You see yourself through the eyes of another. You see yourself as another, and these crosscurrents of sight meet and would cancel in passing through but are stopped to become entwined, tense knots of air.

You are not a woman, as the woman opposite looks at you, and you are not about to imagine her a man. You would wish she were one to make things easier between you.

If only you were a woman, she is thinking. How much easier life could be for both, but the knot of air stays tense between you, and you have to smile because there is no other way to ease and dissolve the tension; you are each as you are, so you step forward out of the circle and hold out your hand. She promptly follows with outstretched hand, and to your surprise, it happens with each person in the circle, each holding the hand of another, a hand no different from your own. You could be holding hands with yourself, but the voice speaking to you is another's, and this difference is what interests you to go on being yourself talking and loving.

■ *43.*

Sadly is how I must say it
because I am one brother
and you one sister. Together
we fade into the crowd
of many faces awaiting our bed.

Should we not become many happinesses,
many starts of love and elated deaths?
My body weakens into the milky dawn
and grows pale with effort. You
already are dressed and moving about,
a person with a coffeepot. I
stick out my tongue to touch
the brightening sky.

■ *44.*

Finally, I have reduced you to a human being.
I have recovered my own humanity,
as you concede quietly. I listen and am sad.
We are two mirrors standing opposite
each other, in one another's reflection.

Where is your first experience
of ruling me with your eyes,
you who must be looking for me
behind my eyes and my reserve
only to find that I am once again
a disappointment, as we are to ourselves.
I am my own small independency
and you the kingdom of yourself.
We meet to form a treaty of respect
and commonality, touching
at the borders of each other's self,
our bodies meeting on a bed.

■ *45.*

The men you've loved are one man,
the women I've known are one woman;
I hold your hand and look
into your face with love, in peace.
We lie down together
and nothing matters
but making each of us
the first and the last.

■ *46.*

What we have done to keep a good house
and an orderly one: loved strangers,
even those who came to muddy up the floors;
loved them in place of commotion,
the sooner to be rid of them
or to find in them a spot
of their own cleanliness—as love
would hypnotize us to believe,
and once rid of those who have gained
theirs in getting love from us, we
cleaned up again: recalled their pleasures
and our discoveries.

All this, taking our strength day after day,
has left us, the central idea, in possession
of a new fact: that we are old in the work:
we falter at the windows
and seek to hire help, friends,
whose payment is to take all.

■ *47.*

Air that embraces me in a gentle breeze
is just as intent at that moment on touching
the lips, feet and arms of the population
of the world. Oh, anybody's whore whom we love,
nevertheless; who makes amoral persons
of us all. Hitler slept with and was touched
by air and every escaped assassin and bank robber,
every double-crossing politician and racist
stretches himself luxuriously each morning
in bed in the summer air through his open
inviting window.

What shall we do with such an indiscriminate
being that teaches us to be unfaithful
to our wives, husbands and lovers,
and that so many of us take as inspiration
to follow our new-found morality
with a passion? As for me, in view of such
practices as air induces, immune to punishment
or retribution or unhappiness with itself,
I lift a hand to caress the cheek
of my own special beloved and dream
large, world-throbbing dreams.

■ *48.*

The glow upon the ground
beneath the tree that lets the sun
come through in spots like light
upon a brown-skinned woman partly
shaded by a tree—she turns to show
her sunlit teeth in welcome
to her lover approaching. She sees him
as a tall stalk of grain striding
above the field. He wraps his leaflike arms
around her waist, and she her sunlit arms
around his neck, and thus they stand
until evening falls, until night fades
into dawn, until the sun rises.

■ *49.*

A leaf spirals directly at the tall grass
without wavering or hesitation, as if knowing
in advance where it must go. And now it lies
hidden in the grass, not stirring, content
with itself, I would say, having left the tree
to find itself a place on earth.

■ *50.*

I did not take into account my disillusionment. I looked to overlook it, to throw myself into new life, and there you were about to be born. Now you are grown and, as it seems, look at me in my guilt, to ask, "Why did I have to be born? Why could I not have stayed with the earth, the clouds, the sun and the moon? Why am I a part of this restlessness, tears and striving for what I do not know?" I can't answer, I have no answer. I could confess myself deluded about the new life I was to start at your birth. You then would mock and call me self-centered, an egotist who thought nothing of giving pain to another. I would have to acknowledge my fault, and you would weep that I am wishing you were never born, and so I would be caught in the irony of not being permitted to tell the truth. I remain silent. I bend my head. I could say, "We'll push through, we'll manage, we'll survive, we'll do everything to make ourselves happy." And you would smile gladly, ready to deceive yourself also. We would be implicated together in the great lie and carry on with humor about ourselves and find reason for living in laughing at ourselves, and so to look at each other in recognition and affectionate contempt.

■ *51.*

How was it possible, I a father
yet a child of my father? I
grew panicky and thought
of running away but knew
I would be scorned for it
by my father. I stood
and listened to myself
being called Dad.

How ridiculous it sounded,
but in front of me, asking
for attention—how could I,
a child, ignore this child's plea?
I lifted him into my arms
and hugged him as I would have
wanted my father to hug me,
and it was as though satisfying
my own lost childhood.

■ *52.*

It is annihilation of the person you became in meeting people who cannot exist for you in your room. You shed them painfully and are frightened, left with the person you were, this with whom you are now, composed of fear and doubt setting you adrift. You are nowhere in particular and do not know that you exist except as these feelings. It is the end of you, become the ocean of your feelings. Fish are in that water: sharks and whales and all other manner of living fins and tails.

Is it a giddy moment for you to have become an ocean in your small, private room? Nothing more can be said until you learn what whales and sharks and other moving fins do in your waters, for they could not exist without your feelings having become oceanic and a nourishment for other life than your lost one—then to have discovered this life in you become a festive occasion.

■ *53.*

The machine, you know, will vary with the weather.
Since iron and steel are products of the earth,
why should they not alter with the atmosphere?
Be kind to your machine, then, as to your dog
or self. In sun or rainy weather do not ask
the same results of it, and do not push it
too far and fast. One tiny screw binding
air rod to valve will break as if by accident
in your hand. Do not believe it an accident
merely, but a warning, and then shut down
the motor, let the machine cool off
and slowly, very slowly, replace the broken
with the new. Be sure the threads are clean,
do not force. Try it gingerly at the tip.
Do not resist if it balks and try again
with another but be careful, be careful
always of this created thing. It knows you.

54.

What's your name?

What does it matter to you?

Because I have a ticket for you.

What kind of ticket?

Well, I can't tell you unless I know your name.

But how can my name have any bearing on the ticket?

Well, it could change with your name.

Are you crazy?

No, my name is Sam.

Then I'm crazy.

Oh, so that's your name. Well, the ticket I have is for you to appear at Bellevue at 3 P.M. sharp to have your head examined.

What for?

Didn't you say you're crazy?

But not that way.

What other way is there?

I don't want to be questioned like this as if I were guilty of something.

Being crazy is not being guilty of anything. It's something you can't help.

Well, I'm not crazy.

Then you were lying.

I was lying.

Then I have a different ticket for you.

What is it this time?

A ticket to come with me to the police station.

What for?

For lying.

Arrest me for lying?

Sure.

Are you a policeman?

No.

Then how can you arrest me?

Because you're interested.

Interested! I'm horrified.

Then that's another name you go by. This definitely needs questioning by the police. You must be hiding something. You must have stolen a watch.

I stole nothing but my patience with you. I've taken too much.

This is a citizen's arrest. Come with me. You have confessed to lying, hiding under a pseudonym and stealing.

■ *55.*

In the spaces between the stars still water dances.
In the clouds of morning the evening is flowing
backward to its evanescence—also meaningless to you.

I had not expected to convey to you my self
in transport in a vision, and now I must start again
to express it in yet another way, as the silent flower
in the silent desert that instantly begins to bloom
more silent flowers, as I am writing this.

Now you are surely in the desert there with me
because no such desert exists. We are
both at a loss. "This is my brother." I am
introducing you to the silent flowers,
and they understand.

■ *56.*

I wish a god were possible,
at least for me, to find myself
content in that knowledge
and as I die believe an immemorial mind
will hold me in remembrance live
and let to walk about
in an eternal sense of self,
as children do, looking up
into the sky, of which they sense
themselves a part, the sky boundless.
Children think so,
and in my wish for god, I am a child,
feeling in myself the wish
that is itself a god
in being boundless.

"The waves laughed as they died."
Because they would be reborn
the moment they died.
They could laugh, like children
free of their parents on the open
streets of their happiness, to be
free to wander as life itself, as death:
two doors, neither of which would be marked,
and it would make no difference
to the children, the surprise to happiness
being to discover later which door
they had left behind
in their wandering.

■ 58.

I am lifted from my sadness
to see everything as a gift
with which to make a life
that I could love
even as I lay dying. This
the religion I've been searching for
and now it is gone into this writing—
simply a hope and hope alone
to me is a reality but not to you
who have yet to feel
the need for hope.

■ *59.*

To welcome the day
from earliest creation
of the world, to spend himself
in adoration, to watch
the day depart in shades of darkness.
To speak of loss and of his faith
in day's return because of faith,
his world closed to evil
in this circle.

■ 60.

In sleep I meet myself
and rise, as if awake,
to ride to work, and smile
at you who in that sleep
too ride with open eyes,
as if awake.

From every side we come
to meet our counterparts
at work asleep
in their ecstatic love
of being.

■ *61.*

He sees the coming and going of friends
and adversaries and smiles to himself
of the secret he contains
of his complicity in living with the world
for he already knows the end
as he has known the beginning
but will live as in the beginning
until the end.

       He is that sort of schemer
and he adores himself as a smooth talker,
a friend to his foe and a friend to his own death.
He is happy without letting it be known
publicly because the odds are
that it would spoil the game of being alive
for to live is to think about it,
to draw conclusions, mainly skeptical
and reserved but to draw conclusions
that are in themselves works of art.

Happiness of that kind, reserved
for the privacy of his thoughts,
except for the others. Who are they?
He does not know but there are others
and they live, they live forever,
as he has been told by instinct
for living. In short, the world is not
about to end with him and there are the others
and he gives them his poems to keep,
as absent-mindedly, distracted by life,
he walks off to his end.

■ *62.*

I've wanted to write my way into paradise,
leaving the door open for others. Instead
I am scribbling beneath its walls,
with the door shut.

What is the magic word?
Is there a magic word?
Am I standing beneath the walls of paradise?
Does paradise have walls?

Friends, strangers and relatives look to me
patiently or with sneers and amused tolerance,
crowding around, waiting for the door to open
at my words, but all I can offer are these
questions. They see me uneasy, seated
with my back against the wall,
my eyes closed to rest, to sleep, perhaps
to dream of the paradise
we were to enter at my words.

■ *63.*

It is wonderful to die amidst the pleasures I have known and so to die without recrimination towards myself and others, free of guilt at my shortcomings, happy to have lived and happy to know death, the last of living, my spirit free to sing as when I felt it born in my youth. The youth of it returns in dying, moving off from anger that racked its throat.

With death before me, I look back at my pleasures and they were you whom I held close in loving, and in the poems I've written for this truth, which is their beauty and lets me die in pleasure with myself. I did not fail my life.

New Poems

I

■ *In Dream*

I died and called for you,
and you came from a distance,
hurrying but impassive. You
looked long and steadily
at my face, then left and strode
back into the distance, rapidly
growing smaller to the eye. You
vanished, but where I lay
I could hear your voice
low and quick, urging me
to awaken to the sunrise
at the window of the bedroom
where we slept together. I
rose up and followed you
into the distance, and there
heard the laughter and wit
with which we had spent
our days together. Then silence,
and I knew we both were dead,
for you had spoken to me
in death, as only the dead
could do, and so at last
we were together.

■ *Concrete*

We roll apart, lie side by side,
quiet. We talk of love, family
and troubles. In silence we regard
each other's life and check the time
for school, trains, schedules,
business calls. Getting dressed,
we take our bodies with us
like heavy bags slung
across our backs. Breakfast is food;
words are conversation; lips kissing
good-by are flesh; cars starting up
to take leave are of metal,
and the road is concrete.

■ *After*

After sex, a couple talks together
to assume an identity,
assuming there is a further
dimension from which interest
starts again in one another.
They then turn away
with an animal need
to eat and drink.

▪ *It Is*

It is heartrending to know a kiss
cannot cure the world of its illnesses,
nor can your happiness, nor your tragedy
of being a discrete man, for the bodies
fall like rain into the ground
and merge only to make an ocean
of bones and closed eyes, our identities
merged, as we had wanted
when we were persons
in each other's sight and touch.

■ *Silently*

What may two lovers say
that is not embarrassing,
deceitful or unhappy
after marriage and divorce
and earlier affairs?
They may say with their tongues
in each other's mouth silently.

■ *I Will Walk*

I study the folds of fat round your waist lovingly, as you bend over naked to slip on your panties. Don't lose weight for me. I don't ask you to add weight either. That would make me a glutton. As you are, with small, protuberant stomach, your buttocks like two halves of the world kept sturdily aloft and apple breasts to feed my eyes, oh, woman of my longing, I see rolling hills endlessly stretching before me, and my heart is lifted that I will walk these hills for my lifetime.

■ The Answer

We are standing in the narrow hallway
upstairs and looking into each other's eyes
and discovering an unknown felt obstacle
between us. I say it is the separate
self in each other, and you say,
Let's go to bed and find out.

■ *The Principle*

Make no mistake, you cannot take
my love without accepting my body,
and you cannot accept my body
without a claim to all that I am
and shall always be, that which
has determined me from my beginning,
in the branches of the rain,
in the blood of animals and trees.
As you take me in your arms,
you are making love to all the world
that I am.

■ *Letter*

I love you, of course, and do you know who else I love? Your mother, your father and, of course, your sister, and then I walk out into the street and I love everybody in sight, but what can I do about it? I can't enter their houses, chanting I love you. Your house is the only one I know at present that will let me in, so let me love you as if you were everybody and I was everybody's lover. It's a fine compromise for today, as long as we know we're not being exclusive with each other. The thing is that as I love you, I do want to feel loved in return. Waiting for your reply, signed,

David

■ *I'm Asking*

I'll build you a house,
you'll invite me in.
I'll cook you a meal,
you'll feed me it.
I'll earn some money,
you'll spend it on me.
I'll write you a poem,
you'll recite it
as addressed to me.
I'll talk to you of love,
you'll demonstrate by kissing,
and so on. Will it work?
We will know shortly
after we begin to try out
my plan, stated above.
I'm asking only
that you start on time
and take the cigarette
out of your mouth.

■ *Were You?*

Were you perhaps sent by the FBI,
CIA or Secret Service? I am so quiet
lately, content without a word
of protest against drug traffic,
rising prices, shrinking dollar
and much more that I fought against
loud and long. Yesterday,
with your legs around my neck
you said, Know what I like about you?
And I asked, and you answered,
Your independence and sociability.

■ *Once More*

An odor passed between us distinctly a fart,
and neither of us spoke, lying in bed
side by side. What was there to say,
once more baffled by life.

II

▪ *The Separate Dead*

The leaves on the tree in front of my house—they live and die together, with subtle shades of green at birth and subtle shades of brown and yellow at their deaths. Everybody stands around to admire them and then each goes about his business in separate houses, beds, tables and chairs, with separate knives and forks and living rooms with separate lovers, husbands and wives, and each dies alone, to be buried separately.

The leaves grow thin and wasted-looking, curl up and fall off the branch by the hundreds, like paratroopers from their planes, silently prepared for the next move.

Those leaves that fall upon the graves will lie mouldering and in the rain-soaked earth turn to moss and add their portion to the ground in which the dead are lying, the separate dead.

■ *In My Childhood*

In my childhood I awoke to my mother's voice
in the kitchen and knew I was someone
cherished, I belonged. I could look out
the window bravely and admire
the silent, drifting clouds
and look down upon the silent street
and lend my presence to give
its character of trees and sky. Everything
existed in itself in my childhood,
as though between the walls of a synagogue
where I could sit identified as the child
who had yet to learn and was willing.

And when I stepped into the street
among the people walking swiftly past me
to business or to their private affairs,
I shrank from the separateness it made of me.
Now as I lie in the breaking dawn,
frightened of the silence around me,
I am fighting panic that everything
does exist in itself alone.

East Side West

The stairs squeak like mice caught outside
their holes. I notice the stained brown door
of my neighbor, perhaps the one whose mailbox
I have envied, packed full like a suckling pig.
The door sounds with life behind it,
the door seems to speak: a mother shrieks
at her youngest daughter, snaps at her next
oldest child, grumbles to herself
of the work, curses the whole bunch around her.
"Kids, kids!" She needs help, lonely for help.
A mother, I recall, of four, her hair
braided around hawk features. Trailed
by these four duckling, she lugs shopping bags
in both hands up five flights. The good husband
every night at six races up the stairs
and his rat-tat on the door demands entrance
into his rightful troubles. The door closes
behind him and begins to sound with a new tune:
money, the bosses, the working conditions,
the other workers. Stinks, all stinks.
He is lonely for help.

I turn the corner to this first floor carefully
so as not to be heard having stood so long
in the hall listening. Up on the next floor
a radio croons with a practiced, honeyed voice.
A young girl moans with it off key.
She too takes care of a house, her mother dead,
one baby sister left behind, four grown brothers
busy on street corners shooting craps.
The baby cries and she snaps at it.
I have seen her look long passing me
on the stairs, as if searching in me
for the help she needs.

■ *Proem*

Is a tree guilty?
Can water be condemned?

The house was built for shelter where people could stand upright without fear and talk openly and bravely to one another of the moment in the security of four walls that provide a stage, a place to act in, to be oneself exclusively, to become known, honored, loved, needed and looked to. In short, an ideal relationship, love at its center, beauty its objective, with confidence and trust in the other, with belief in what a house stands for, locking out thievery, murder, betrayal, deception, dishonesty and faithlessness towards the other—in this way placing the divergent, the strange, the aberrant, the unsought-after and, even more, making these unhappy, sad, confident or pleased act to preserve such a house: all that is in a tree to do for itself because it too is a life being lived for the sake of living; that too is in the water, each born of the urge to be born and to live for the sake of being alive. But that tree is splitting the foundation of the house; that water is inundating the basement, crumbling the masonry of the walls. So then, who is the guilty one?

The house will fall apart, the people will scatter to save themselves, and they will accuse each other of negligence, oversight, self-centeredness and arrogance. Is the water guilty? Is the tree to be condemned? Is the world a place in which to accuse one another of the guilt of living? Is there something to being born that is wrong? Is it wrong then to want to live? Is it wrong to live?

◾ *A Phase of Order*

Could I calmly watch myself being robbed of my wallet,
slashed with a knife to answer carefully that this is the
working out of an order unto its wholeness; that my body
suffering its wounds is a metaphor of the earth stripmined, laid
bare; that with time and with others will be made fertile again?

I being myself and filled with suppressed rage tell myself this
is the working out of the wholeness of order, just as the body,
ill and near death, works out its wholeness in recovery or in
death; that my face and neck wounded, my purse stolen manifest
a phase of order in disorder.

■ *Nothing*

Nothing is left but the stars
to look at and wonder on.
Human life is no longer
a mystery, as it sinks
into a dead star. What
is left are the bright ones
from afar.

■ *Wait*

I am a man and do not know why I was born. I can tell you the facts: my mother conceived me when my father lay with her, but that is not what I'm asking about. Why did they think it was necessary for me to be born? I can understand love and the desire to have something to show for it, but should I live on that promise, my parents buried? For whom now should I live when I am dying, as did my parents who left nothing of themselves but me who am about to die? If there is anyone with an answer, let him or her step forward. I am patient and can wait.

■ *I Write*

I write to capture the meaningless as it were an animal in the thickets to hold in my arms; my identity in this animal which, since it exists for me, gives me my reality too. Whitman, I am happy to say, turned inside out, having found the answer to his answer, and away I go, cutting through woods and across fields and rivers back to cities with a shout of absolute terror. Why? Because here the meaningless exists too, ready to kill me with a knife or a bullet or a crazy drug. So I shall be killed, and I will weep in my grave, missing the meaningless.

Trough

I'll watch that mailbox as if it were an ikon of some religious order about to bring me a blessing from another world. After lunch, I'll sit back on the sofa which faces the window and look out from time to time, lifting my eyes from the daily press and, when the mailman appears and spends the first few moments in sorting out my mail from the others, my heart will quiver. And when I do open the letters, I'll find I'm back with people, side by side, as at a trough, eating our way through life out of each other's hands.

■ *And Now*

That's my corpse you're looking at, laid out as I've in-structed, with hands clasped before me as in prayer and just a bit of color in my cheeks, my lips pressed firmly together, yet revealing their soft, appealing curve, with something of a smile there in it, my head raised slightly upon a pillow somewhat above the level of my chest. All in all, I'm satisfied, and I hope you too like it, my friends, who have been so patient and loyal through the years of my depression, and so you see now that my thoughts weren't always on despair but on ways also to please you, taking me out of myself.

And now let us gather around the body and sing the songs of my youth that were so precious to me, romantic songs without a truth in them; songs that took me from my somber self. Sing but a few and look at each other for the signs of love or their likeness in each face transported, not with pity and terror and not with fervent wish to be free of it all, as I am. Then bury me and let me go my way deep down into the earth to become one, at last, with the others before me. Be careful how you place me in the box, to return me to the earth whole, without blemish, for the earth was good to me, and I would give myself back in good condition.

■ *The Meeting*

Strange, but I get the impression that you're dying.

Oh, do you mean my sallow complexion, my sunken cheeks?

Yes, and also your eyes are dull and unmoving.

Oh, that, and so perhaps I am

Then let me say farewell for now.

Of course, but why for now?

Because I'll be joining you one day.

Well, I see no signs on you.

None, except that I keep looking for signs in others, which could mean the onset in me already has begun, simply by my becoming aware of dying—a kind of gentle hint it could be.

True, and I have thought so about myself, and now you tell me it is true, and so it already has happened, in my features particularly.

So it goes.

And when will we meet again? In this world, I mean. And by the way, what is your name?

I am in the telephone book.

And so thanks for stopping me in the street, as you've just done, to tell me my condition, as you see it.

No thanks at all. I would hope I'd have the same courtesy done to me one day.

Yes, I was not sure what was wrong with me, but thanks again, for now I know.

And let us see each other, if possible.

Yes, after work could be nice for dinner. What did you say was your name?

Of course, for dinner.

And see you soon.

See you soon.

■ *The Interview II*

I represent *The Morning Shout*. We hear you are dying. May we interview you before you pass on?

Certainly. There won't be another such another opportunity, I'm sure.

We'd like to know what you will miss most, at your death.

Music, nothing but music. Classical and popular, if someone or an orchestra will play during my last hour. I'll be very thankful.

Are you happy to be passing on?

Well, I'm of two minds about it. One, I'd like to hang on a bit longer and, on the other hand, if I can't, I'd like my passing on to be considered an event of some importance.

Next question: Do you have any regrets for having lived as you did? Is there anything you would have done differently if you were given a second chance?

Oh, yes. I'd like to have said hello to my parents more often rather than ignoring them, as I did, even as a young man. I'm sorry about that.

Is there something you can say you are proud of having done in life that you would do over again if given the chance?

Oh, yes. I enjoyed making lots of money, and I'm very proud of having left a fortune. It was a pleasure to accumulate, and I'd gladly do it again, especially to see my name listed in the Obituary, with mention of my wealth. Excuse me, I think I'm beginning to sink rapidly. I will have to say good-by to you for now.

One last question: What are you experiencing at this moment in passing on?

Oh, a slight headache and a feeling of missing out on something. Good-by.

Finally: Are you dead and, if so, can you describe it for us, for your admiring public.

No comment.

■ *The Spirit*

If you will say the sea is water,
I will concede,
or that the world is earth,
I will nod.
From these affirmations I draw
whatever cheerfulness I can
as that which should be the portion
of a well-deserving man. I give myself
these airs by smiling and nodding,
since everything else I could contribute
I have lost. I have the spirit
which seeks out its substance.

■ *The Image*

The image in the mirror feels nothing
towards him, though it is his image. He
weeps, and it weeps with him, but is merely
the sign of his weeping, yet he knows
he cannot eat, drink or make love
without that image. He is in awe of it.

Though it does not need him,
he is its servant as he stands there,
doing what is necessary
to keep it in the mirror—humbled
and grateful for its presence,
that which reveals him to himself.
If there is a god, this is he.

Also by David Ignatow

Poems
The Gentle Weight Lifter
Say Pardon
Figures of the Human
Earth Hard: Selected Poems (1968)
Rescue the Dead
Poems 1934–1969
The Notebooks of David Ignatow
Selected Poems (1975)
Open Between Us (prose)

About the Author

David Ignatow has published thirteen volumes of poetry, a prose collection, and his *Notebooks*. He has received two Guggenheim fellowships, the Wallace Stevens fellowship from Yale University (1977), and the Rockefeller Foundation fellowship (1968). His awards include the Shelley Memorial (1965), and others from the National Institute of Arts and Letters (1964), the National Endowment for the Arts (1970), and the Bollingen Prize in 1973. He is visiting professor at New York University and Columbia University. He lives with his wife, Rose Graubart, in East Hampton, New York.

About the Book

The typeface used in this book is Galliard, a contemporary rendering of a classic typeface prepared for Mergenthaler in 1978 by the British type designer Matthew Carter. The book was composed by Graphic Composition, Inc., of Athens, Georgia; it was printed on 60-pound Sebago and bound by Kingsport Press of Kingsport, Tennessee. The design is by Joyce Kachergis of Joyce Kachergis Book Design and Production, Bynum, North Carolina.

Wesleyan University Press, 1986